Charles
A Prince of our time

Judith Campbell

OCTOPUS

Contents

First published in 1981 by
Octopus Books Limited
59 Grosvenor Street
London W1

© 1981 Octopus Books Limited

ISBN 0 7064 0968 X

Produced by Mandarin Publishers Limited
22a Westlands Road
Quarry Bay, Hong Kong

Printed in Hong Kong

Endpapers: Prince Charles romping with his young cousin Lady Sarah Armstrong-Jones, then aged eight, on the hill at Balmoral. This 24th birthday picture vividly captures the Prince's *joie-de-vivre* and love of children and the open air—all part of his charm.

Previous pages: Suitably attired for a day in the country, the Prince goes riding at Badminton.

Opposite: The royal line of succession traces back directly to William the Conqueror, and even beyond that to the ancient Royal House of England. But one of the most important links in the chain of Prince Charles' inheritance, and of particular significance for his position as Prince of Wales, was forged with the succession of Henry VII, the first sovereign of the House of Tudor. The king was of Welsh descent and the representative of the House of Lancaster (red rose). He married Elizabeth, heiress of the House of York (white rose), which gave their descendants an unchallengeable right to the throne.

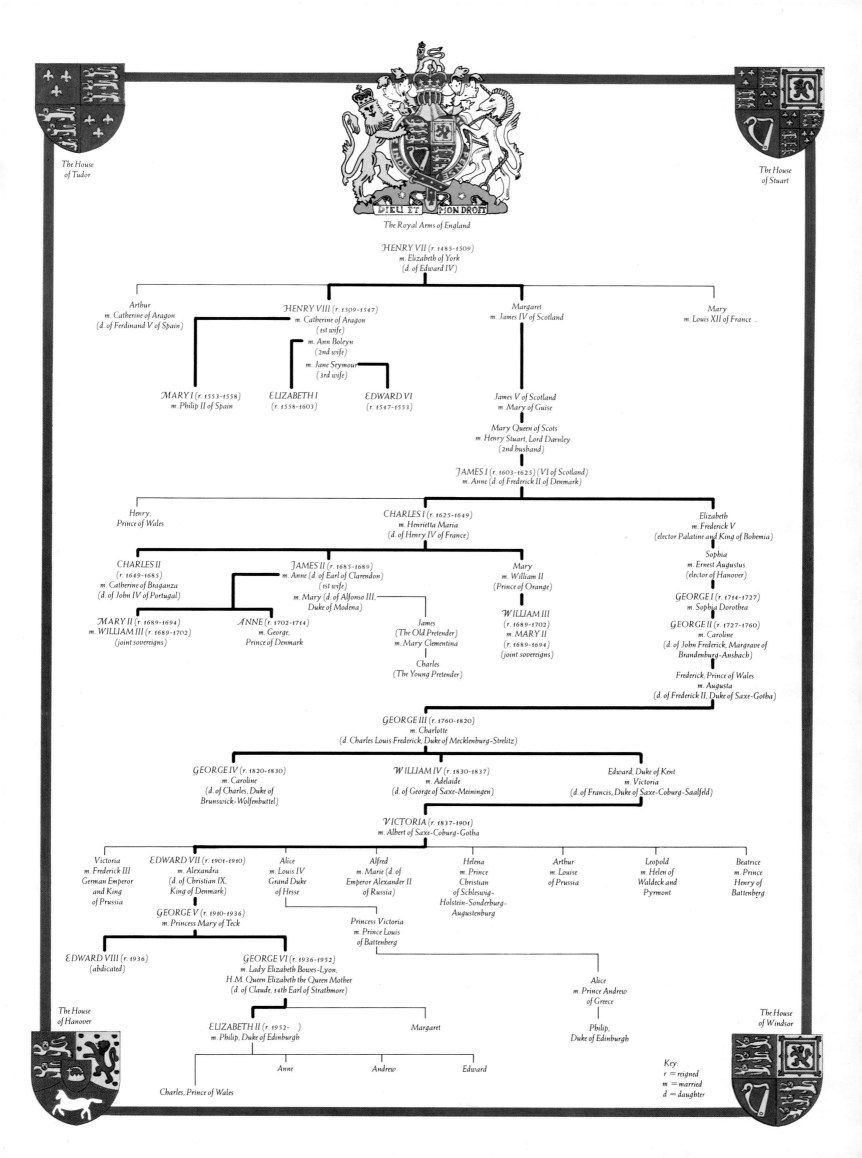

The House
of Tudor

The House
of Stuart

The Royal Arms of England

HENRY VII (r. 1485-1509)
m. Elizabeth of York
(d. of Edward IV)

Arthur
m. Catherine of Aragon
(d. of Ferdinand V of Spain)

HENRY VIII (r. 1509-1547)
m. Catherine of Aragon
(1st wife)
m. Ann Boleyn
(2nd wife)
m. Jane Seymour
(3rd wife)

Margaret
m. James IV of Scotland

Mary
m. Louis XII of France

MARY I (r. 1553-1558)
m. Philip II of Spain

ELIZABETH I
(r. 1558-1603)

EDWARD VI
(r. 1547-1553)

James V of Scotland
m. Mary of Guise

Mary Queen of Scots
m. Henry Stuart, Lord Darnley
(2nd husband)

JAMES I (r. 1603-1625) (VI of Scotland)
m. Anne (d. of Frederick II of Denmark)

Henry,
Prince of Wales

CHARLES I (r. 1625-1649)
m. Henrietta Maria
(d. of Henry IV of France)

Elizabeth
m. Frederick V
(elector Palatine and King of Bohemia)

CHARLES II
(r. 1649-1685)
m. Catherine of Braganza
(d. of John IV of Portugal)

JAMES II (r. 1685-1689)
m. Anne (d. of Earl of Clarendon)
(1st wife)
m. Mary (d. of Alfonso III,
Duke of Modena)

Mary
m. William II
(Prince of Orange)

Sophia
m. Ernest Augustus
(elector of Hanover)

GEORGE I (r. 1714-1727)
m. Sophia Dorothea

MARY II (r. 1689-1694)
m. **WILLIAM III** (r. 1689-1702)
(joint sovereigns)

ANNE (r. 1702-1714)
m. George,
Prince of Denmark

James
(The Old Pretender)
m. Mary Clementina

WILLIAM III
(r. 1689-1702)
m. **MARY II**
(r. 1689-1694)
(joint sovereigns)

GEORGE II (r. 1727-1760)
m. Caroline
(d. of John Frederick, Margrave of
Brandenburg-Ansbach)

Charles
(The Young Pretender)

Frederick, Prince of Wales
m. Augusta
(d. of Frederick II, Duke of Saxe-Gotha)

GEORGE III (r. 1760-1820)
m. Charlotte
(d. Charles Louis Frederick, Duke of Mecklenburg-Strelitz)

GEORGE IV (r. 1820-1830)
m. Caroline
(d. of Charles, Duke of
Brunswick-Wolfenbuttel)

WILLIAM IV (r. 1830-1837)
m. Adelaide
(d. of George of Saxe-Meiningen)

Edward, Duke of Kent
m. Victoria
(d. of Francis, Duke of Saxe-Coburg-Saalfeld)

VICTORIA (r. 1837-1901)
m. Albert of Saxe-Coburg-Gotha

Victoria
m. Frederick III
German Emperor
and King
of Prussia

EDWARD VII (r. 1901-1910)
m. Alexandra
(d. of Christian IX,
King of Denmark)

Alice
m. Louis IV
Grand Duke
of Hesse

Alfred
m. Marie (d. of
Emperor Alexander II
of Russia)

Helena
m. Prince
Christian
of Schleswig-
Holstein-Sonderburg-
Augustenburg

Arthur
m. Louise
of Prussia

Leopold
m. Helen of
Waldeck and
Pyrmont

Beatrice
m. Prince
Henry of
Battenberg

GEORGE V (r. 1910-1936)
m. Princess Mary of Teck

Princess Victoria
m. Prince Louis
of Battenberg

EDWARD VIII (r. 1936)
(abdicated)

GEORGE VI (r. 1936-1952)
m. Lady Elizabeth Bowes-Lyon,
H.M. Queen Elizabeth the Queen Mother
(d. of Claude, 14th Earl of Strathmore)

Alice
m. Prince Andrew
of Greece

The House
of Hanover

ELIZABETH II (r. 1952-   )
m. Philip, Duke of Edinburgh

Margaret

Philip,
Duke of Edinburgh

The House
of Windsor

Anne

Andrew

Edward

Key:
r = reigned
m = married
d = daughter

Charles, Prince of Wales

A Royal Childhood

Above: Most young children enjoy tooting a trumpet but with Charles it augured a little more than that. When he was older he learned to play both the trumpet and the 'cello, and although for some years there has been no time for such occupations, music remains an important ingredient in his life.

Right: The Queen and Prince Philip did their best to keep their children out of the limelight for as long as possible. Charles was a shy boy, and there were certainly phases when photographers were not his favourite people!

Prince Charles is often asked what he would have liked to do in life if he were not who he is. His reply is predictable. He thinks it would be very difficult to do—even to visualize—any job other than the one for which he has been trained and of which he feels an integral part. There are innumerable other professions, but there is only one heir to the throne.

His Royal Highness Prince Charles Philip Arthur George, Prince of Wales and Earl of Chester, Duke of Cornwall, Duke of Rothesay, Earl of Carrick, Lord of the Isles and Baron Renfrew, Prince and Great Steward of Scotland, is in direct line of descent from William the Conqueror and a great-great-great grandson of Queen Victoria. Born at Buckingham Palace on 14th November 1948, he is the first child of Her Majesty the Queen and His Royal Highness the Duke of Edinburgh. At the time, his grandfather King George VI was on the throne, and his mother, then Princess Elizabeth, was the heir presumptive.

The King was only 53 and it was reasonable to assume it would be many years before his daughter, let alone his grandson, would accede to the throne. But, as far as anything in life is certain, one day, however far in the future, the baby Charles would become King Charles III of England. What kind of king he would make, how he might deal with the duties and responsibilities, the demands and restraints of the monarchy in a rapidly changing world, what kind of man as well as prince he would become, depended to a large extent on the manner of his upbringing.

To begin with, apart from being brought up according to the high principles that govern both the public and private lives of the Queen and Prince Philip, there was no specific training for the role. Charles' parents were determined that he and any subsequent children should have as normal a childhood as possible. It remained to be seen to what extent the restrictions, outside pressures and requirements of protocol inevitably connected with the children of the reigning sovereign could be lightened.

The Queen, up to and even after 1936 when her father reluctantly became king, had had a freer and far less formal childhood than would have been conceivable to a member of any previous British royal family. But although she and her sister Margaret were brought up in a very happy and affectionate atmosphere, the Princesses' existence was still very sheltered compared with the life of other girls of their generation, and it was made more so by growing up during the war years. Their life was very unlike that of Prince Philip, the man Elizabeth was to marry.

By inheritance a prince of Greece, by blood a prince of Denmark, and with an English mother (a granddaughter of Queen Victoria), Philip was born on the Greek island of Corfu, on 10 June 1921. Scarcely a year later, after his uncle King Constantine I of Greece had abdicated for the second time, Philip's

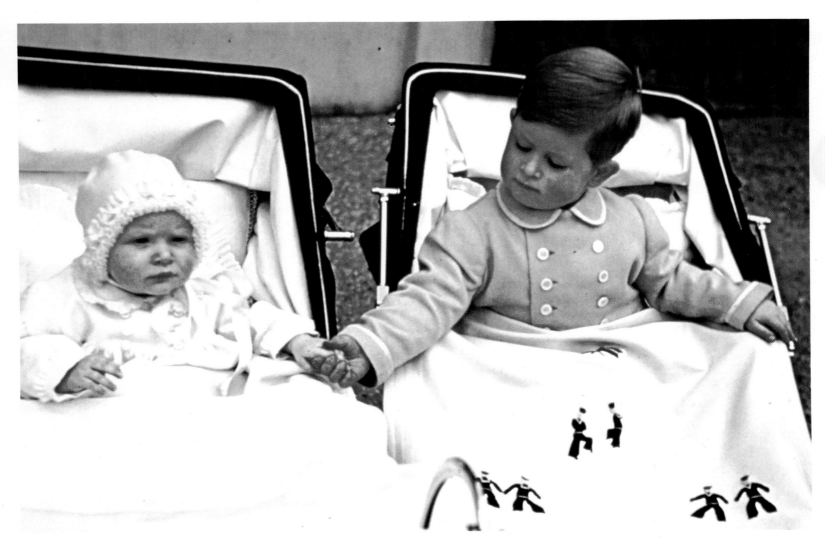

Above: At three years old Charles was taking a great interest in his baby sister Anne, who was born at Clarence House on 15 August 1950.

father Prince Andrew, narrowly escaping with his life, fled with his family to exile in France. There Philip, seven years junior to the youngest of his four sisters, developed into a tough, active and independent boy, his self-reliance increasing with the years as his parents drifted apart and England eventually became his adopted homeland.

As they looked back, there was plenty from their own childhoods for Charles' parents to adapt to their son's rather different circumstances and to the different attitudes of the times in which he was born.

In the summer of 1949 the Edinburghs moved from their temporary apartments at Buckingham Palace where they had lived since Charles' birth, to Clarence House, the home just off the Mall where Princess Anne was born in 1950. Here Charles and his sister lived much the same nursery life as other young children of well-to-do families of the time. True, there were a few exceptions. When the children were taken for a walk into Green Park or St James's Park, there was always a plainclothes policeman unobtrusively in attendance, and, if recognized, the entourage might have to retreat to the walled garden at Clarence House. There were no formalities with their parents, but as a small boy Charles was taught always to bow when greeting his great-grandmother Queen Mary or his grandparents the King and Queen. As quite young children, Charles and Anne were encouraged to wave to members of the public who waved to them, a pastime that seemed to appeal more to the extrovert Anne than to her brother. There was nothing then about the daily routine to give Charles any idea he might be 'different'. Considering the demands of their public lives and work after the Queen's accession, and contrary to what many people assume, the Queen and Prince Philip always managed to spend a great deal of time with their young children.

For a short while after the King's death in February 1952 there were no apparent changes in Charles' life, and the family continued to live at Clarence House. But after the Easter holiday that year, as usual spent at Windsor Castle, the children were brought back to the nursery suite at the Palace. The Queen

Right: Military ceremonial is an integral part of royal life, and to play a drum like one of the Guardsmen Charles watched from the nursery windows was one of his earliest ambitions.

Mother and Princess Margaret made their home at Clarence House.

At the Palace, nursery life continued largely unaltered until Mabel Anderson, originally employed as undernurse, took charge. (She is now nanny to Princess Anne's own baby.) Under her commonsense rule, the basic nursery routine was unchanged, and the same standard of good manners, thought for others and obedience was instilled. Any traces of extra formality due to Charles' changed status soon gave way to the same relaxed, happy atmosphere the children enjoyed with their parents. Their everyday clothes—the jeans and jerseys that their contemporaries were wearing—reflected this informality.

Despite their parents' wish to keep the children in the background, there were obviously occasions when they did appear in public. Charles watched a short part of his mother's coronation in Westminster Abbey, a concession that, because of her youth, was denied his young sister and that for years enraged her with its apparent injustice. On ceremonial occasions both children usually joined the Queen and Prince Philip on the Palace balcony. As soon as they were old enough, they accompanied the Queen Mother to Trooping the Colour. They attended Craithie Church when at Balmoral, and the annual Highland Games at Braemar. And these were the times when Charles as a small boy was more predictable than his sister, with an apparently built-in awareness of what was required of him.

Unlike the adventurous Anne, a born ringleader to the extent of appearing bossy, Charles was very shy and unsure of himself. Both children were very affectionate, and in some ways Charles could be self-contained, but normally he was dependent on other people. He did not enjoy amusing himself, much preferring such alternatives as seeking out one of the Queen's ladies-in-waiting to chat with while she sorted the letters. Anne, perhaps subconsciously resentful of being a girl and the younger of the two, and feeling somehow of less account than her brother in their first nanny's eyes, was so determined to keep up with her brother that she appeared completely self-sufficient.

Below: This toy horse and carriage was a great favourite with Charles and then with his sister. After their mother became Queen and they moved to Buckingham Palace, the long passage outside the nurseries proved an excellent place for trundling it and other toys around.

Although so unlike in temperament, Charles and Anne have always enjoyed each other's company. They squabbled frequently in the nursery, and continue to argue, if with good temper, about most things, but they share the bond of the same sense of humour. Since growing up, they have acquired a totally dissimilar circle of friends and interests but have a shared liking for speed, physical exertion and life in the open air.

There has always been a special rapport between Charles and his grandmother, the Queen Mother. He has said that 'all she touches turns to gold', and they never seem to lack subjects to talk and laugh about together.

Like many sons, Charles adds a specially close relationship with his mother to the deep love and respect he has for both his parents. For years he longed to be just like the father he so admires, and now there is an unmistakable resemblance, the adventurous delight in having a go, the way they stand and walk, the same gestures, quick laughter and humorous asides. But as a young

Below: It is of course impossible to keep royal children entirely out of the public eye, and when the Queen took them with her Charles, for all his shyness, seemed to have an inborn sense of what was required of him.

Above: All the royal children have been brought up to enjoy the pleasures of the countryside regardless of weather, and appropriately sensible clothes for rural occasions were part of the Queen and Prince Philip's down to earth outlook in bringing up their family. Here rain and muddy conditions did not spoil the royal family's appreciation of the annual Three Day Event at Badminton.

Right: 'I am often asked why my father and I have this habit. It is not a genetic trait, as some people think, but because we both have the same tailor. He makes the sleeves so tight we *cannot* get our hands in front!' Prince Charles' joking explanation for a posture he first adopted as a boy, made in recent years when guest of the Master Tailors' Benevolent Association.

boy Charles seemed to have little of Prince Philip's expertise and quick grasp of a subject, and the ability to do things easily and well did not come naturally to him. By nature Charles was a slow developer, less spontaneously rumbustious than his sister in the nightly frolics with their parents at bath and bed time, more diffident in outdoor games and excursions.

As Buckingham Palace is basically the work centre of the Royal Family, when in London the children had to stick to a fairly rigid timetable for seeing their parents. The Palace is where the bulk of the work is done, but an appointment had to be of uncommon importance to interfere with the times set aside each day for enjoying family life together. And the Queen and Prince Philip always did their best to keep the school holidays clear of state and other visits abroad.

Most weekends, and now Christmas, are spent at Windsor Castle which belongs to the State. For their summer holidays the family go to Balmoral in Scotland—the castle that Queen Victoria built and loved so well—and for a few weeks after Christmas they stay at Sandringham House in Norfolk, which, like Balmoral, is the Queen's own home. In these homes the children spent most of the time with their parents and were brought up to the country life that both the Queen and Prince Philip prefer.

The Royal Family's private life is mostly very simple, lived as much as possible in the open air, totally regardless of the weather, and the main rites scarcely changing with the years. This life includes dogs—the corgis and other small dogs that travel with their owners, and the labradors, the Queen's gun dogs kept at Sandringham and Balmoral. There are also always horses, over and above the Queen's racing bloodstock and the various animals she breeds at Sandringham. In London there are the state carriage horses that inhabit the royal mews, while the Windsor mews now house Prince Charles' polo ponies and the riding animals, some of which go on holiday with their owners. The Austrian Haflingers, and the Highland and Fell ponies that are bred on a small scale at Balmoral, were another source of interest to the children.

Each home produced its own pastimes. One of the favourite occupations of Charles and Anne at Windsor was playing about with a boat on the lake at Frogmore, with tea afterwards at Royal Lodge, the Queen Mother's country home in the park. Visits to the home farm, which, like the Sandringham estate, is run as a commercial proposition, were popular and engendered that feeling for the land that flavours many of Charles' interests. In early summer the children spent most Sunday afternoons at Windsor up at Smith's Lawn, watching Prince Philip play polo, helping the Queen stomp in divots between chukkas and, when they were old enough, giving a hand with the ponies.

Windsor was where the Queen taught both children the rudiments of riding with the aid of a loaned Shetland pony, and when Charles was eight they acquired a pony of their own. He enjoyed riding this and subsequent ponies but was never as dedicated or as talented as Anne. As with most boys, the chores attached to looking after ponies did not appeal to him and, unlike his sister, Charles was seldom to be seen around the mews unless he was actually riding. From time to time both children were given professional instruction and they became members of the Garth Pony Club. When Charles was about 12 they shared a good Welsh pony called Bandit and both competed at pony club level with quite a lot of success. But when this pony was outgrown, Charles' enthusiasm waned—a process possibly hastened by the unsolicited advice from a younger sister who was better at riding than himself.

Wherever the Queen may be, state papers are sent to her daily. At Balmoral, once the work is finished, the Queen is out and around the estate with Prince Philip, or she joins him and their guests in the butts for a grouse shoot, or employs her skill in the arduous art of deer stalking. Even when quite tiny, the children were included in their parents' frequent picnics at Balmoral—something they still do as often as possible, the family barbecueing their own meals in remote spots away on the hill to which Queen Victoria used to drive with an entourage of carriages. Sometimes Charles and Anne would help their parents wooding and clearing scrub. There were big bonfires to build and tend

and, at dusk, songs to sing around the leaping flames. There is always plenty to do outside at Balmoral and Sandringham.

Although Sandringham is a very big house, it is now not big enough for a full family gathering. But for Charles this cosy country home that, like Balmoral, is marvellously remote from public life, always spelled the enduring rituals of Christmas. It was there that Prince Philip taught his son to handle a gun at an early age and, with an eye for the sport said to be as good now as his father's, Charles was soon included in the pheasant shoots. The family went beachcombing on the shore at Holcombe, playing boisterous warming-up games by the sea just as they do today. In the evenings, as they sat around the big log fire, there were hotly contested rounds of racing demon or canasta, and sessions of that disconcerting form of charades called 'The Game' favoured by the Queen, in which Charles first revealed his inherent talent for acting. There was the mounting excitement as the clock moved on to Christmas Eve

Below: All the Queen Mother's grandchildren vote her a super grandmother, and she and Charles have always been on a special wavelength of understanding. Here they are attending the 1957 Horse Trials at Badminton, the estate of the Duke of Beaufort.

and Christmas Day, the big tree sparkling with lights, huge mounds of parcels for everyone in the house and on the estate, matins in the little church and the singing of familiar carols.

Charles began his formal education when he was five and, because of his shyness, the Queen thought it would be easier for him to be taught alone in the Palace schoolroom with his governess, the late Miss Peebles, rather than with a group. Other children were included in his visits around London to places of interest, and were sometimes invited to come and play with him in the afternoon, but, used to the constant stream of visitors to the Palace, Charles tended to prefer the company of adults and was far more forthcoming with them than with his own age group.

Contrary to all royal precedent, the Queen and Prince Philip considered it essential that Charles should go to school. He started at Hill House (then a pre-preparatory school) when he was eight. It was gentle breaking in, his two terms shortened first by a furore of publicity that prevented the new boy starting at the beginning of term, then by tonsillitis. Hill House did little to cure Charles of his selfconsciousness with his own age group. It was not that he had any idea of status—he seems to have been scarcely aware of his special position and the other boys were themselves too young to be bothered with such things— but he was excessively shy.

Scholastically, it emerged from his short sojourn at Hill House that he had no great enthusiasm for learning, but was a conscientious trier. He could read and write quite well and showed some promise at French. As a subject, geography had come alive for him to some extent at the age of five, when the Queen and Prince Philip had gone on a six-month world tour that took them to ten Commonwealth countries. History had not yet been recognized as the source of learning about his own ancestry. Arithmetic was already the bugbear it was to remain throughout his academic career—a fact that caused the Queen more sympathetic amusement than dismay.

Charles loved to sing, and best of all to draw and paint—an inheritance from Prince Philip whose artistic talent provides one of his most enjoyable relaxations. With the exception of polo, team games have never held much appeal for Charles, but the running and jumping that comprised Hill House athletics did.

In actual schooling none of this amounted to much, or was intended to, but in those few weeks Charles had taken the first hesitant steps in communal education—and, what was much more important, one of the few possible steps towards a goal that in its entirety was fundamentally impossible: experiencing the life of an ordinary person. To give to the heir to the throne the complete life and upbringing of an ordinary boy is a contradiction in terms. Protocol, privilege and precedent can be, and were, put aside to a degree, but by parentage and background, by virtue of being who he is and the unique nature of the job for which he is training, Charles could never be ordinary, either as boy or man.

As a child, Charles was never baldly informed that he must do this or not do that because his mother was Queen and he was the heir to the throne. At his parents' wish, as far as was practicable everyone in the household tried to treat him as the small boy they all called Charles. But by the autumn of 1957, when he started as a boarder at his father's old preparatory school, Cheam, he had a growing awareness of who he was and of the future, which he eyed with some foreboding the clearer it became. This knowledge added to the miseries of a very homesick nine-year-old, who had left Scotland for Cheam with an ominous sense of apprehension.

The Queen well understood Charles' distress at leaving home, and there must have been moments when she was tempted to revert to home tuition for her son. But neither the Queen nor Prince Philip make important decisions lightly, or balk at carrying out what they have decided is right even if it is against personal inclination. Both wished for Charles what, since he has been of an age to make his own decisions, he himself has done his best to further: attempting those things most likely to make him competent for his mission in life.

Below: Charles on his way to Craithie Church, where the royal family worship when at Balmoral. It is not easy to define the Queen's exact position as head of the Church, but she attends divine service each Sunday wherever she may be, and has brought up her family to be conscientious and practising Christians.

School and University

Above: At Fort William in 1961. The seeds of Charles' subsequent decision to serve in the Royal Navy were probably sown on those enjoyable excursions with his father and sister around the Scottish coast.

Right: By November 1968, when this 20th birthday portrait was taken at Windsor Castle, Prince Charles had just completed the first of his three years at Cambridge University.

Prince Charles recalls the time at Cheam as the most difficult of his growing-up years, but if he never really got over his homesickness and the embarrassment of his position, he was still as resilient as most children. He covered up well, became as forthcoming in making friends as his natural reserve allowed, and conscientiously made the best of an experience that at least in the latter part became more enjoyable.

Again Charles was not rated as any great scholar, but he had a lively intelligence and, understandably, a wider range of general knowledge than is usual with children of his age. Music was becoming increasingly important to him. He was still not showing his father's aptitude at cricket and football, but swimming was another matter. Prince Philip taught all the children to swim in the heated pool at Buckingham Palace, and Charles took to the water like a fish. He still goes swimming as often as possible.

There was one marvellous happening during those years at Cheam—a family affair—the birth of Charles' brother Andrew in 1960. Charles was to be well into his time at public school when Edward was born four years later to complete the family, but, even when they were babies, he took the happiest interest in his young brothers. Now time is quickly bridging the generation gap between them and until Andrew went into the Navy they spent a good deal of time together. Charles and Andrew seem to share the same adventurous spirit and capacity to enjoy life, especially when in each other's company.

With Andrew and Edward, the general public have seemed less prone to give the Queen and Prince Philip all the gratuitous, and often contradictory, advice proffered over the upbringing of Charles and Anne. There was not much public excitement over Andrew's advent at Gordonstoun—if considerably more about that attractive young man's date of leaving school. But there is still occasional speculation about whether it was a good or bad idea to send Charles to Prince Philip's old public school, and usually the most important point has been missed.

Charles was not *sent* to Gordonstoun. There was consultation at family and ministerial level, but, in line with the Queen and Prince Philip's consistent policy once their children are old enough to make sensible decisions, Charles was given the pros, cons and alternatives, and then the chance to make up his own mind. His reasons for choosing Gordonstoun were mixed, and probably not entirely clear to himself. As the unwilling recipient of press and public attention during his early days at Cheam, he must have been attracted by the inaccessibility of a school beside the Moray Firth, north-east of Inverness. But the chief reason for his choice in those days would have been the urge—for years one of the mainsprings of Charles' character—to try to follow in his father's successful footsteps and prove himself to himself on the same ground.

Above: There are not many public occasions when the royal family can enjoy themselves almost as freely as private citizens, but their annual outing to the Three Day Event at Badminton is one where, by tacit agreement with the enormous crowds who flock to the beautiful estate, they are able to do so. Prince Charles has been enjoying these horse trials since he was quite young, and as a schoolboy is seen here with the Queen and Princess Margaret taking a keen interest in the cross-country section.

The school, based on the principles of Kurt Hahn, is not the regimented body-building cult of some people's imagination, but it is a little out of the ordinary. It is dedicated to producing 'complete men, with practised hands and alert, cultivated minds', and is geared, through service to others and physical adventure and exertion, to providing boys with the means of finding out at an early age how to meet both triumph and defeat.

Gordonstoun's atmosphere, activities and opportunities were exactly suited to Prince Philip's vigorous, penetrating personality, to his absolute involvement in everything he undertakes and to his outstanding flair for leadership. Long after, his son was also to 'find himself' to a great extent during his years at the school. Charles responded to the amenities of mountain and sea, which are used extensively at Gordonstoun for physical and moral training, and to the occasional solitude offered by the place. But with his different, more gentle personality—the same unexpected core of toughness possessed by his mother, tempered with her serenity and concern for individuals rather than his father's directness and practicality—the going was considerably tougher for Charles.

On balance, the choice of school was a good one. Charles was never school-minded, but he is the first to acknowledge the benefits school conferred on him. Other considerations apart, it was at Gordonstoun that he at last shed much of his shyness, and it was through the self-discipline and valued experience of responsibility gained there that he achieved some much-needed confidence in himself and his own abilities.

In 1964 Charles obtained satisfactory passes at 'O' Level in Latin, French, History, English Literature and English Language. After another period of determined plodding he was able to add two more passes to the list—much to his satisfaction, in the unpalatable subjects of Mathematics and Physics. But the educational experience that was to have the greatest effect occurred two years later in January 1966. That was when Charles was 17 and exchanged his place at Gordonstoun with an Australian, for two terms at Timbertop, the upcountry section of Geelong Church of England Grammar School, Victoria.

The boys Charles would be mixing with were younger than himself but, like most young Australians, mature for their age. Timbertop has a similar approach to Gordonstoun, but has less classroom education and the boys are expected to study principally on their own initiative. There is even more emphasis than at Gordonstoun on developing self-reliance and fending for oneself. The work Charles was doing in preparation for his 'A' Levels had to be continued more or less on his own and fitted in with the round of daily chores the boys have to undertake to keep Timbertop going.

All in all, the object of the exercise was not academic in the accepted sense but was to provide a valuable opportunity for education in one of the most important aspects of kingship: the knowledge of people as individuals. Timbertop was equally important as a means of enabling Charles to get out on his own and establish his growing self-confidence.

He did not feel very confident as he flew out to Sydney in a Qantas Boeing 707 jet. He was accompanied by Squadron Leader Checketts, on loan from Prince Philip, but who then became Charles' equerry and private secretary until May 1979. The squadron leader was to live 100 or more miles from Timbertop, acting as a kind of liaison officer dealing with the public

Below: A moment of informal relaxation that comes all too rarely in a busy life.

relations side of the enterprise, and, with his wife, providing a home base for Charles when he was not at school. A metropolitan police officer was seconded to watch over the Prince's physical safety, but otherwise he was really out on his own two feet—and distinctly apprehensive at the prospect. He had heard that Australians could be critical and were not backward in showing what they felt. He was wondering what on earth he should do if they disliked him. Within a few hours of landing he had most of the answers to his forebodings.

The Australians were both welcoming and friendly. They came up without reserve to talk about anything they wanted to, and he liked their naturalness as much as he was to like their country. At Timbertop the boys were a little wary at first, due partly to the age difference, partly to Charles' own innate reserve, the old holding back in case people were more interested in his rank than in himself as a person. He need not have worried. Within days the heir to the throne was being encouraged by comments of 'Good on you, Charlie!' as he laid tables for meals, cleaned out pigsties, or sawed up gum trees for fuelling the hot-water system.

The environment, the buildings laid out on mountain slopes and the gum forests that surrounded them, was much to Charles' taste. He quickly learned the accepted rule for happiness there: to fill each minute of each day, voluntarily or not, with work, play, daily chores or physical effort. The unaccustomed heat, the dust and the flies added to the exertions of such Timbertop specialities as Inca racing—where teams of 15 boys each heaved a heavy log over a mile course. There were compulsory weekend hikes, and a four-day 70-mile marathon through the Australian Alps, on which the boys lived mostly out of tins because of the danger of forest fire.

Most of the programme was designed as exercises in the art of self-preservation and in the comradeship that shared adventure breeds. Some of it was rough, tough and physically exhausting, but for Charles each day brought its own exhilaration and challenge. There is still a glint of pure enjoyment in his eyes when he mentions that first visit to a country to which he returns whenever he can. There is no doubt of the truth of his own comment that he 'absolutely loved it ... the most wonderful experience'.

During the short break between the two Timbertop terms, the Prince and his equerry were able to travel around some other parts of the continent. In the years since, he has travelled literally thousands of miles visiting innumerable different countries, but that opportunity to get to know a bit more of the world and the people in it when he was young and impressionable, as he says, 'made the whole difference to my outlook'.

The Australian interlude ended in July 1966. In September Prince Charles returned to Gordonstoun to pick up the threads of a school life from which he had in many ways grown away, and to continue working for his 'A' Levels. He had matured, his horizons had developed and expanded and he was ready for a less restricted experience of life. But first this new-found assurance brought him the position of Helper (captain) of his house, and in the following term that of Guardian (head boy) of the school, a position that carries no more, or less, respect than that merited by its holder. The honour was well earned.

Before leaving school, achievement in first aid, pottery and athletics, together with the initiative shown on an expedition in the Cairngorms, qualified Charles for a silver award in the Duke of Edinburgh's Award Scheme. 'A' Level passes in French and History, with scholarship level in the special paper in History, prepared Prince Charles for the next step forward, life as an undergraduate.

The choice was Cambridge, where the late King George VI went in 1919. The college was Trinity, of which Lord Butler was Master and which had been founded by Henry VIII.

Queen Victoria sent the genial but unacademically inclined Prince of Wales to three universities, without either turning him into a scholar or allowing him participation at ordinary level in any university activities. The late Duke of Windsor, when Prince of Wales, went up to Oxford complete with personal tutor, equerry, valet, and his own bathtub. His life there did not resemble that of his grandfather, but he did remain fairly firmly under parental control.

Left: Prince Charles at work in his study at Cambridge, May 1969. During his time at university there were occasional royal duties to perform, and he worked harder than most students of his year. Otherwise he was able to live the life of an ordinary undergraduate, which included getting around on a bicycle, cooking the odd snack for himself, and sometimes buying food in the local market.

During Prince Charles' three happy years at Cambridge his personal detective was living unobtrusively in Trinity College. From time to time, the Prince was absent on royal duties; he spent a term in college at Aberystwyth, he was invested as Prince of Wales, and towards the end of his time he travelled abroad. Otherwise, he lived the life of an ordinary undergraduate and enjoyed every minute of it.

The Prince first read Archaeology and Anthropology. He then switched to History, another favourite subject, achieving a Second Class Bachelor of Arts degree. This automatically qualifies the holders for the Master of Arts degree, in this case conferred in 1975. These results may have surprised some, but not his tutor—although, because of outside distractions, Charles did have to work harder than average.

Despite this, he found plenty of time for vigorous debating in the Cambridge Union, playing polo, dancing, making music, and successfully continuing to indulge his talent for acting.

Back in London he had his own amusements and girl friends. Like Anne, he still breakfasted in the nursery, always dropped in to say good morning to the Queen and Prince Philip, and then came and went at will. Life was good.

Left: Charles was able to expand his talent for acting while at university. He is here rehearsing for one of the Cambridge revues, in which he figured prominently and exploited his liking for slapstick.

Left: The Prince having a discussion with Dr Dennis Marrian, the fellow of Trinity College who, as his tutor, gave him guidance and counsel in his university life. When Charles left Cambridge part of Dr Marrian's assessment of him as an undergraduate was that he 'has a great capacity for getting his head down and studying really hard when he has to'.

The Prince of Wales

Above: In 1969 Charles was invested as Prince of Wales, at a ceremony that since 1616 has only once before been performed in public—and that was in 1911 for the investiture of the Prince's great-uncle, the late Duke of Windsor.

Right: The first full-length portrait of HRH the Prince of Wales, painted by Leonard Boden and commissioned by the Worshipful Company of Painter-Stainers. Painted at Buckingham Palace, the portrait shows the Prince wearing the Garter Robes over RAF uniform, and hangs in the Painter's Hall.

In 1301 the prerogative of bestowing the title of Prince of Wales was taken from the Welsh by force of arms and since then has usually, but not automatically, been bestowed on the eldest son of the reigning sovereign of England. With the honour goes that of the Earldom of Chester, the oldest of the dignities of the heir apparent and one that, unlike the Duchy of Cornwall, which is entailed by charter, merges with the crown when the holder becomes king.

When his mother became Queen, Charles became Duke of Cornwall in his own right, but the Queen did not wish to create him Prince of Wales until he was old enough to understand at least some of the implications of the title. She waited until the 26 July 1958, when Charles was nine and in his first year at Cheam. Then he listened on the school radio to the Queen's message to the Welsh people, recorded because of illness, and given in Cardiff at the closing ceremony of the British and Commonwealth Games. His mother's words confirmed what he already knew, that the Queen had decided to create her son Prince of Wales that day, and would present him to the Welsh at Caernarvon when he was grown up.

The crowd roared their appreciation and sang 'God bless the Prince of Wales', applicable again now that there was a holder of the title after a gap of 22 years, while Charles, pink with embarrassment amongst his schoolmates, realized hazily that this was the real start of the work for which he was being trained.

As Prince of Wales, Charles also became a Knight of the Garter, the oldest secular order of chivalry in Europe, founded by Edward III. But he could not occupy his knight's stall in St George's Chapel at Windsor or wear the magnificent Garter insignia until the Queen had dubbed him knight. That ceremony was still ten years in the future, preceding the investiture in Wales by a year.

As the prelude to the investiture in 1969, Prince Charles became Colonel-in-Chief of the newly formed Royal Regiment of Wales and just before the ceremony spent a term at the University College of Wales at Aberystwyth.

Through the Queen Mother, Charles is descended three times over from Welsh princes, but this bore little weight with the small but militant faction of Welsh nationalists opposed to the investiture. There had been bombs as well as bomb hoaxes and a hunger strike of protest at the University College, and the Prince arrived there not certain what to expect. He felt he could scarcely blame any Welshman for being unenthusiastic about a so-called English prince arriving in their midst. In fact, the investiture was to pass off almost without incident, and Charles' term at college was uneventful—if rather lonely, because there was so much work to fit in. The Prince had come to Aberystwyth to imbibe as much as he could of the history, people, cultural and political problems of

Right: It was estimated that in addition to those lucky enough to be present, five hundred million television viewers all over the world watched the investiture of Prince Charles as the twenty-first Prince of Wales. The ceremony, a three-hour programme and the first state occasion to be televised in full, was planned by the Earl Marshal, the late Duke of Norfolk, and beautifully staged by Lord Snowdon as Constable of Caernarvon Castle.

Far right: Except for the religious service and the presentation of the Prince to the people of his principality, both innovations introduced in 1911, the ceremony of investiture has hardly varied through the centuries. Kneeling before his Sovereign, Charles was invested with the insignia—the sword, for the defence of his land, the coronet, an emblem of principality, the ring, representing responsibility, the rod, a symbol of government, and the mantle. The Prince then did homage and exchanged the kiss of fealty with the Queen, before being led to his seat on the right-hand side of the throne.

Wales, but one of the objectives of his stay was to learn as much Welsh as was possible in so short a time. Welsh is a very difficult language, but Charles was determined to do better than the few 'parrot phrases' most people expected of him. Aided by a good ear and the family penchant for mimicry, he gave a 300-word address to a critical Welsh League of Youth audience. At his investiture, he replied not only in English to the loyal address from the people of Wales but in moderately fluent Welsh delivered with a good accent.

That mastery of their language was more appreciated by the Welsh than any other gesture of goodwill. It was also an illustration of the conscientious outlook that Prince Charles has inherited from both the Queen and Prince Philip, the painstaking thoroughness over what they call their 'homework'.

This first investiture of a Prince of Wales for 58 years, and the first held inside the now roofless walls of Caernarvon Castle for six centuries, was beautifully staged yet relatively simple. And next to the Coronation, it was the most impressive ceremony of Elizabeth's reign to date. It was a moving moment when Charles knelt to do homage to the Queen for the Principality of Wales and Earldom of Chester, using the same sincere oath of allegiance that his father had addressed to his mother at the Coronation 16 years before.

All big public ceremonies must create some degree of tension for the principals, and the Royal Family are not alone in welcoming incidents of light relief to combat the solemnity when it is all over. After the investiture, Prince Charles, accompanied at the start by Princess Anne, was to set off on a tour of Wales. They were driven off to Holyhead in the Queen's big Rolls-Royce, in which neither had ever been before without their parents. Sitting there side by side, with the roof down to give a good view, they could have been a pair of young newlyweds setting off on their honeymoon—a resemblance that seemed to amuse the Queen as much as the couple concerned.

In the spring of that year of 1969 Prince Charles had made his debut on radio in an interview at the Palace with Jack de Manio. It was an important occasion, an introduction of the heir to the throne of whom the majority of people knew very little, and it was a success. Charles sounded as sincere as he was unassuming, and possessed of an engaging sense of humour. To be natural on radio or television has never been a problem for him—even on the tricky day when a technical hitch necessitated repeating a 'spontaneous' interview, with 'off the cuff' answers to much the same questions.

Just before the investiture, Britain and the Commonwealth, and in particular Wales, had the opportunity to learn more of Prince Charles during an hour-long recorded talk with David Frost on BBC television. Again he impressed, and not purely as a first-class subject for the medium. The delivery was important, but it was the subject matter that was most important.

Apart from his obvious involvement with Wales and the Welsh, there was no mistaking this young man's sincere desire to be of service, to become involved with people, even if at the time he was still uncertain how best it could be done. There was acceptance on his part that his training had to be unique, and realization that the 'organization' to which he belongs is certainly no longer taken for granted as it used to be. He felt that the principals needed to be professional as never before, much more 'with it', much better informed. The outmoded word 'duty' featured in that talk, but the point was made that if he, as Prince of Wales and heir to the throne, did not have a real feeling of duty towards the United Kingdom and the Commonwealth, then his job became meaningless.

Charles sounded engagingly young, but there was more than a hint of the Prince who has since emerged as a man who is genuinely concerned about the big issues of the world and who does his best to do something about those within his compass. The trouble is there are few guidelines to the work of a Prince of Wales. Skill at arms, valour and strategy on the field of battle were the chief attributes demanded of that medieval Prince of Wales popularly dubbed the Black Prince. And maybe Prince Charles, a self-confessed romantic who frequently hazards his neck and, while hating war and everything it means, still wishes he had experienced the last one, would have worn the Black

Left and below: The Queen Mother and Prince Charles attend the ceremony of the Order of the Thistle at St Giles' Cathedral, Edinburgh. This Order, second only to that of the Garter in the Orders of Chivalry, was instituted by James II in 1687, and revived in 1703 by Queen Anne.

Prince's suit of armour with equal distinction.

Charles' great-great-grandfather, King Edward VII, was denied constitutional responsibilities when he was Prince of Wales and dissipated much of his lengthy apprenticeship to the throne. But he did manage to turn his love of travel to good account. Somehow he persuaded Queen Victoria to allow him access to all Foreign Office dispatches. Then, and after he became King, through his journeyings he helped to retain the semblance of European peace and—what appeared most unlikely—was partly responsible for establishing the *entente cordiale* with France.

The late Duke of Windsor, as Prince of Wales, travelled 150,000 miles around the world, performing his role as ambassador for Britain to good effect, and was greatly acclaimed. Before he revealed the aspects of his character that made him set personal inclination before public duty, and before in the eyes of many he became an example of how not to treat the trust of monarchy, that Prince of Wales was for thousands of people a man of much promise.

Prince Charles is a strong believer in retaining the best of tradition. He is also a student of British history, and when he was young he was fascinated to discover that the subject covered the story of his own ancestry. And now, grown to be his own man, he can take what he likes of the past and adapt it to fit in with his own ideas on the subject of the monarchy.

Training for Kingship

Above: Parachuting may be an unusual sort of training for a future king, but it is one of the disciplines that Prince Charles accepts as a highly qualified pilot. It is also something that he thoroughly enjoys, and in 1977 he took a refresher parachute course at Gloucester.

Right: Wearing the bearskin and uniform of Colonel of the Welsh Guards, Prince Charles, accompanying the Duke of Edinburgh, attends the Queen at the annual ceremony of Trooping the Colour on her official birthday. He rides half a length behind the Sovereign's horse, the traditional position of the Heir to the Throne.

Down through the ages, dynasties have come and dynasties have changed hands, and, in the past 50 years or so, most of them have gone. That the British monarchy survives is due partly to the regard in which the majority of people in Britain and the Commonwealth hold it as an institution, partly to the sterling characters of its more recent sovereigns. But the throne to which Prince Charles is heir wields no direct power. The doctrine of the Divine Right of Kings was thrown out by the Act of Settlement of 1701 and replaced by an Act rigorously limiting the authority of the throne and handing over the sovereign's executive powers to Parliament.

The Queen therefore 'reigns without ruling'—although she can exert her influence in many ways. She has close contact with the Prime Minister throughout his or her term of office, and has the right, which is always exercised, to be consulted on all affairs of state. She can, and does, give her own views, and, with the accumulated wisdom of the years laced with her own good sense, the Queen advises, encourages and occasionally warns. She is entitled to discuss the business of their departments with other ministers. She studies Cabinet papers, Foreign Office dispatches, Commonwealth High Commissioners' dispatches and a daily summary of parliamentary proceedings. With the years, the Queen has acquired an uninterrupted knowledge of events and people in high places that is invaluable to each incoming government.

As hereditary head of the British state and the symbolic head of the Commonwealth, the Queen provides a focus of loyalty that is divorced from, and unaffected by, the battles of party politics going on below her. No transitory president, however powerful, can provide the same emblem of stability as a monarch claiming a continuity of sovereignty going back nearly 1500 years.

A proportion of the Queen's work as head of state is taken up by performing the time-consuming, colourful ceremonial demanded by a nation that, despite changing opinions and outlook, remains devoted to tradition and the pageantry of the past. There are also all the state visits and Commonwealth tours that have proved the Queen and Prince Philip such excellent ambassadors, bringing trade and benefit to Britain in their train.

All this constitutes something of the work and duties that Prince Charles will one day inherit. But there are many other facets to, and advantages of, the monarchy, which, although substantiated beyond doubt, are, since Britain has no written constitution, difficult to define. By another reign, some may be different: in an age of increasingly rapid change, even as honoured and traditional an institution as the monarchy undoubtedly has to change to some extent in order to survive.

The Queen and Prince Philip and their advisers are well aware of this, but the problem is to determine how far to go. Too little change, and the monarchy

Previous pages: Prince Charles was following a long family tradition when he decided to serve with the Royal Navy, and an added bonus to those happy years was the chance to fly with the Service. His strong taste for the air is in line with that of his father, and he shares the same natural ability whatever the type of aircraft. After promotion to the rank of Acting Lieutenant, in 1974 he underwent a three-month course of helicopter training at the Royal Navy Air Station, Yeovilton, in Somerset. His aptitude proved well above average, and he completed 105 flying hours, acknowledged to be 'quite a hard flying rate'. In 1975 he served with an operational helicopter squadron in the carrier HMS *Hermes*, and had the honour of leading the flypast celebrating the tenth anniversary of 707 Squadron.

Right: A love of adventure and the liking for trying his hand at most things, proving the man behind the Prince, have taken Prince Charles into some potentially hazardous situations. Here he is about to attempt walking below the five-foot Arctic ice at Resolute Bay in Canada's far North.

Right: The Prince roars with laughter at his 'Michelin-man' appearance after returning from that particular enterprise! The special diving suit, a necessity as protection from the intense cold, is swollen with the compressed hot air used for insulation, and he is sporting a bowler hat 'planted' for him to find way down below on the sea bed.

could become too remote from the times to retain credence. Too much, and it could become too commonplace for a nation which, while wanting its sovereign to possess the 'common touch', still expects its king or queen to keep sufficient exclusiveness to preserve the mystique surrounding the throne.

During the Queen's reign, a great many changes have been made—and not only in modernizing the communications and amenities of a magnificent and enormous palace, which Prince Philip has described as a cross between a museum and a tied cottage. Since 1956 the more snob functions—the presentation parties, state balls and levees—have been replaced with informal lunches and cocktail parties for interesting people from many walks of life. The 8,000 guests invited to each garden party are chosen more for their services to the community and Commonwealth than for their ancestry. The popular 'walk-about' is firmly established. But for all this, when Prince Charles and Princess Anne began leading their own lives, they had to adjust from the very different 'outside' world, where they found most of their friends and amusements, to 'inside' where the changes can only go so far.

This was in 1969—a time when the Queen and Prince Philip were noting, with some natural pride and their usual down-to-earth outlook, all the head-lined enthusiasm with which their elder children's emergence into public life was being greeted. The Duke, tongue in cheek, attributed their news value partly to the discovery by press and public that the two young people were both attractive and normally intelligent!

Strictly speaking, Prince Charles' public life began in 1965 while he was still at school, when he came from Gordonstoun to a garden party at Holyrood House in Edinburgh, to meet young people from the Commonwealth. At 18, when for purposes of the Regency Act he became of age, he was made a Counsellor of State and so became one of the six members of the Royal Family, headed by Prince Philip and the Queen Mother, who act for the Queen when she goes abroad.

By October 1969 the newly invested Prince of Wales was giving much serious thought to his rapidly increasing duties as heir to the throne, but in that October he had to return to Cambridge to complete his reading for his degree.

In February 1970, sponsored by the Duke of Kent and the Duke of Beaufort, Prince Charles took his seat in the House of Lords.

A month later he obtained his private pilot's licence. Prince Charles belongs to the age of flying, and even without the incentive of a father who takes to the air whenever he can, it would be his natural, indispensable and most enjoyable mode of getting around.

When the Queen was heir presumptive, it was Prince Philip who broke through the now seemingly archaic embargo on her flying the Atlantic. They

Above: Prince Charles in his capacity as Colonel of the Welsh Guards, an appointment held by Prince Philip for nearly 22 years. In a farewell address to the regiment his father said, 'My son is the only person to whom I would willingly hand over.'

Right: Prince Charles learned to fly while still at Cambridge, instructed by Squadron Leaders Philip Pinney and Richard Johns using a Chipmunk trainer. He had already flown solo by the time he joined the RAF College at Cranwell in March 1971, to learn advanced flying and eventually gain his Wings as a pilot with 'particular flying abilities'.

were to represent the King on a visit to Canada, but his illness delayed their departure until it was too late to go by sea, and Prince Philip seized the opportunity to overcome the opposition and fly. The Queen and he have been flying around the world at intervals ever since.

Prince Charles' flying career began in 1955, when he and Princess Anne were taken up in a helicopter for a buzz around over Windsor. A month later they came back from Balmoral in a Viking aircraft of the Queen's Flight. As a child, Charles took as a matter of course the red helicopter that his father has for years been taking off and landing near Smith's Lawn in Windsor Park— just occasionally to the consternation of the horse the Queen might be riding not too far away.

When Prince Charles began learning to fly he took to the medium with the same 100 per cent enthusiasm with which Princess Anne embarked on eventing (competitive horse-riding), and he showed much the same aptitude. The thought of his first solo flight gave him a few 'butterflies in the tummy', but owing to bad weather the actual challenge did not occur until a day in January 1970. That was when the Prince's New Zealand instructor, Squadron Leader Pinney, taxied the Chipmunk Trainer to the end of the runway at Bassingbourne RAF Airfield, climbed out and delivered the ominous words: 'You're on your own, mate!'

There was the moment of wondering if he could do it, the usual vision, if he did manage to leave the ground, of being unable to land again and going on round and round until the fuel ran out. Then he took off, became airborne, and, finding the aircraft lightened of his instructor's weight, was quickly flying better than ever before. He found the entire episode, including getting safely down to earth at the first attempt, 'absolutely marvellous'. Like father, like son.

By the spring of 1971 the Prince had good reasons for deciding to go into the services for a while, but he was not influenced solely by feeling it was a logical next step forward after gaining his degree at Cambridge in the previous June. He has a firm, if unfashionable belief in the importance of discipline, chiefly self-discipline, as a virtue that gives shape and form to the lives of young people. His stock-in-trade is people, how to deal with them, live with them, be disciplined by them and so in turn learn how to administer discipline. There is no better way of learning these things than by training with one or another of the services, in Prince Charles' case first with the Royal Air Force and then a longer sojourn with the Royal Navy. But even then, and although the narrow confines of a ship at sea provide the best possible means for learning about people, it was no great surprise that the Prince of Wales' service with the Royal Navy was limited to five years.

A modern-day king cannot be too much of a specialist. He has to be a man of many parts, and the Prince, who has described himself as a 'jack of all trades', appreciates the point. He also appreciates that during the time he has as heir to the throne it will be considerably easier for him to move around, do the things and make the contacts he will need in the future, before that future arrives. However much he may enjoy the different aspects of the things he does, however worthwhile they are, he cannot become involved for too long. As heir apparent he has to move on, or at least until he feels his range of knowledge is sufficiently wide.

Prince Charles flew to the RAF College, Cranwell, in March 1971, to begin a five month shift as a flight lieutenant, accepted at that rank as a Graduate Entry One Group. Tradition—his grandfather King George VI served with the RAF for three years from 1919—had something to do with the Prince's choice, but mainly it was to further his love of flying and the above average talent he has for the art.

The examination that had qualified Prince Charles to hold a private pilot's licence had encompassed aviation, law, flight rules and procedures, meteorology and an oral test, all taken under the supervision of RAF instructors. He had completed 80 hours' flying in the Chipmunk (part of the time solo) and rounded off with a further 10 minutes solo in a Beagle Basset. He was then qualified to fly any single-engined aircraft under 12,600 lbs unaccompanied.

At Cranwell the Prince began his training on a 400 mph Jet Provost under the instruction of Squadron Leader Dick Johns. He progressed to Phantom bombers, and co-piloted the new Nimrod anti-submarine jets. There was a lot to be packed into those few weeks with the RAF, and not all of it concerned flying and the concentrated, fearsomely technological knowhow that is needed for dealing with modern aircraft.

There was no difficulty, just as there was to be none in the Navy, with establishing himself as a junior officer—in both cases, unpaid at his own request. Those who served as brother officers with the Prince of Wales in either service are as unanimous in commending his correct, friendly and unassuming behaviour as those who had the task of commanding a future king—and just might have found it a bit of a problem.

Prince Charles says that he is 'stupid enough to like trying things', and that usually means something that is not strictly obligatory and involves some degree of risk. When he was in the services it could have been interpreted as meaning he liked to undertake the same hazards as anyone else. While at Cranwell he became the first heir apparent to make a parachute descent. After splashing down into Studland Bay he acquired the taste for parachute jumping that sent him on a refresher course at RAF Brize Norton, Oxford, in 1978. The course took place a week after Prince Andrew had been there, having a go at the same sport at novice level. Judging by their same expressions of exhilaration after landing, jumping out of aircraft is a pastime that has equal appeal for both brothers.

Wherever he may be Prince Charles leavens most nonserious working moments with his own brand of humour, and Cranwell was no exception. There was plenty of shared laughter and jokes in those weeks, and one satisfyingly successful April Fool's Day hoax. There was also much to add to his expanding experience of people.

And when the weeks came to an end, Prince Philip was at the passing out

Left: The Prince of Wales sports casual clothes for casual occasions, but is always correctly turned out for the more formal events—in this case driving a pair of Windsor Greys at Smith's Lawn, Windsor, in the *concours d'elegance* during a meet of the British Driving Society.

Below: The Royal Welsh Agricultural Show in North Wales, in 1973. With his interest in the countryside, attendance at this type of show is one of the royal duties that Prince Charles finds particularly engaging.

Above: The Prince inspects a contingent of the President's Guards in Ghana in March 1977. During that year of the Queen's Jubilee Prince Charles travelled extensively, starting with Ghana where he was the first member of the royal family to arrive since the Queen's state visit of 1961.

parade, watching with pride as Air Chief Marshal Sir Dennis Spotswood pinned the coveted Wings to Prince Charles' Garter Sash, and handed over the 'above average' citation that went with them—well earned rewards on completing the 12-month course in 5 months. That was the end of what the RAF had codenamed 'Golden Eagle'; it was another milestone passed in the training for the future, but it was not the end of the Prince's flying with the services.

There were very strong traditional reasons for Prince Charles joining the Royal Navy. His great-grandfather King George V, his grandfather King George VI, and his great-uncles, the late Earl Mountbatten of Burma and the late Marquess of Milford Haven were all naval officers of distinction. Prince Philip joined the Navy in 1940, went to sea on active service during the war, and only left a career he loved because of the King's illness and subsequent death.

The Prince began his naval career in September 1971 by taking a six-week course at the Royal Naval College, Dartmouth, with the rank of acting sub-lieutenant, his curriculum including 'man management', marine and electrical engineering, and the navigation and seamanship in which he passed out top. Once again it entailed cramming a lot of work into a little time.

In November 1971 Prince Charles flew to Gibraltar to join his first ship, the guided-missile destroyer HMS *Norfolk*, and spent the next five weeks at sea. It was not his first sight of Gibraltar and it was certainly not a first acquaintance with the ocean.

In 1954, when Charles was six, he and Anne made their first voyage in the royal yacht, *Britannia*, when they sailed to Tobruk to meet the Queen and Prince Philip returning from their long Commonwealth tour. Gibraltar was a port of call on the home journey and Charles has a vague recollection of the antics of the famous Barbary apes. But his and Anne's clearest memories are of the sailors' kindness and the couple of little models of the yacht which they pedalled about the deck.

Left: During his service with the Royal Navy the Prince was able to carry the flag to many countries in the world. He is seen here wearing naval tropical uniform (with the rank of Commander) on a sun-drenched beach on the Ivory Coast, the Republic of West Africa.

For the children, this was a first experience of the freedom and fun that combines with the Royal Navy's traditional hospitality to make days on board *Britannia* special for all the Royal Family. They sometimes begin their summer holiday in Scotland with a cruise up the west coast. Even then, there is a daily helicopter to bring in state papers for the Queen. But otherwise those few days at sea mean no formality, no need for 'best behaviour', no publicity —only active games of deck tennis or hockey and lovely hours of doing nothing.

With Prince Philip's naval background, messing about in boats with the children was likely to be a favoured holiday occupation. As the family is in two groups, with ten years between them, their father has had opportunities for this kind of fun twice over, sailing small boats on the Scottish lochs first with Charles and Anne and then with Andrew and Edward. But the younger boys missed out on the expeditions which Charles and Anne had made in the yawl *Bloodhound* because the vessel was sold in 1969.

In *Bloodhound*, if time permitted during the summer holidays, Prince Philip, with a crew consisting of his treasurer, an ex-petty-officer sailing master, and an able seaman from *Britannia*, used to take Charles and Anne on carefree explorations of Scotland's west coast and the lovely areas around Campbell-town and the Caledonian Canal. They spent leisurely days cruising from one spot to another, having picnics ashore and just hooking up somewhere to spend the night. There were additional diversions, of which whizzing about in *Bloodhound*'s rubber dinghy, with its powerful outboard motor, was a favourite with the two youngest members of the party.

The last holiday with *Bloodhound* was spent sailing for eight lovely days up and down the Norwegian fjords, a welcome aftermath to the formality of a supposedly 'informal' visit with the Queen to Norway. The freedom of these interludes was always intoxicating, and despite being of an age to have started their round of public engagements, Charles and Anne spent much of the time playing absurd games of 'tag', chasing around the deck like a pair of puppies.

The sea was part of Gordonstoun life too, and therefore no strange element to the Prince of Wales when he took up his first naval posting in 1971. During the next five years he was to sample the sea in all its moods, from a flat tropical calm off Antigua to a full-blooded Atlantic gale. And like many sailors, he usually suffered the miseries of seasickness for the first few days each time he put to sea.

In addition to HMS *Norfolk* and his own command, the minehunter *Bronington*, the Prince served aboard the coastal minesweeper *Glasserton*, the Leander-class frigate *Minerva*, the survey ship *Fox*, the frigate *Jupiter*, and the aircraft carrier *Hermes*. In all these postings, his conscientious acceptance of duty commanded respect, while his good humour and attractive sense of the ridiculous made him a popular member of the ships' companies. There was no room for even a shred of the old inhibiting shyness. There was plenty for developing that sincere interest in the other man's life and point of view that is one of the ingredients of Prince Charles' likeable personality. He has said that in a position of responsibility or command, to get on with people and to get them to carry out instructions willingly, it is very important to be 'honest and genuine', never 'artificial'. He found that a sense of humour and the ability to give as good as you get were essential. They are good qualities and should have presented few difficulties to one who already possessed them.

However complete Prince Charles' life was as a naval officer, as always he also had constitutional duties to perform. There were such matters as representing the Queen abroad, usually for a country's independence celebrations or at the funeral of a foreign statesman.

In June 1974 he made his maiden speech in the House of Lords. Accompanied by the late Earl Mountbatten of Burma, he was present in February 1975 at the coronation of the King of Nepal, a ceremony of great magnificence staged at Katmandu. In May 1975 the Queen installed him as Great Master of the Most Honourable Order of the Bath, a high order of British knighthood that was founded in 1725 and based on the 'Knights of the Bath' created at the coronation of Henry IV in 1399.

In line with normal procedure for graduate entrants 18 months after entry to the Royal Navy, Prince Charles had been promoted to acting lieutenant in March 1973. His progress along the usual course of naval service was good, and during those years he did not neglect any suitable opportunity for 'trying things'. Soon after joining *Norfolk* he had taken part in an 'escape' from a simulated submarine supposedly trapped on the sea bed. It entailed coming up through 100 ft of water, travelling at 7 ft per second while breathing air caught in a hood over his head. Despite the fact that the operation took place in a tank and there were trained lifesavers present, the risk was sufficient to warrant the Queen's and the Prime Minister's consent to the enterprise before it could take place.

By mid-1974 the Prince was at Yeovilton, Somerset, undergoing a three month course of helicopter training. 'A model pupil and a natural pilot' and 'has a natural aptitude for flying and genuinely loves it' were two comments by the Prince's instructor, who had reason to be proud of his pupil for completing 105 flying hours in 45 days. It was no mean achievement and he was awarded the prized Double Diamond trophy presented to the student on the course who makes the most progress.

The Prince is an excellent pilot, and he always manages to keep calm.

Below: At Katmandu for the coronation of King Birendra of Nepal in 1975, Prince Charles with Lord Mountbatten, whose brutal murder by the Provisional IRA in August 1979 deprived the country of a great man and the Prince of a much valued friend where disparity in age was of no account.

Left: One of Prince Charles' most engaging attributes is his sincere interest in the other person's viewpoint. It was a facet of his character that went down particularly well during his 1977 visit to the USA.

Below: After morning service on Christmas Day at Windsor. Like all close-knit families the royal family and as many of their relatives as possible love to spend Christmas together. Sandringham, the traditional home for Christmas, is no longer large enough, and Windsor Castle has for some years taken its place.

On the course at Yeovilton he was flying solo when one of the helicopter's engines caught fire, but his emergency landing in a field was faultless. But Charles is also humanly fallible. There is a story that he had a near miss with another aircraft over Sussex when he was flying his father. And his staff were more than thankful that their pilot's skill and luck did not desert him when he landed the royal Andover on one wheel at São Paulo airport, Brazil.

With his love of both flying and the sea, it was predictable that Prince Charles' service as an officer in the Fleet Air Arm should have been a highlight of his naval career. And he has special regard for the invigorating 'top notchers' who take off and land high-speed aircraft on carriers. In 1975 he himself served in the carrier *Hermes* with an operational helicopter squadron. And the day after making his first solo deck landing, the Prince, personal pennant streaming from the winchwire, led a formation of 16 helicopters trailing coloured smoke in a flypast celebrating the 10th anniversary of 707 Squadron. In 1977 he was to achieve another pinnacle of personal ambition, by successfully flying a Phantom naval aircraft from the flight deck of the famous old aircraft carrier *Ark Royal*.

While with *Hermes* Prince Charles had the chance of another adventure that was much to his taste. The ship visited the Arctic, and when she was in

Resolute Bay he inspected the Undersea Research Centre and watched a demonstration of walking upside down on the ice under the sea. Here was something that had to be tried, and he lowered himself through the ice into water temperatures that without the safeguard of an insulated rubber suit would have killed him in three minutes. The hazardous attempt at walking was only partially successful, but it was another cause for contentment to someone who enjoys adventure for adventure's sake.

In February 1976 Prince Charles was given his own command, the mine-hunter *Bronington*. At only 360 tons, she was not very large, and, being flat-bottomed, she rolled atrociously in most seas. But as her commander, the Prince had overall responsibility for the safety and efficient running of his ship, and for the discipline, wellbeing and contentment of the five other officers and 34 ratings who made up her complement. The command was a brief one, as Prince Charles left the Navy, with the rank of Lieut-Commander, to return to civilian life in December that same year. It was in fact even shorter than that of Prince Philip who, before he had to leave the sea, had had a year with what was also his first and last ship, HMS *Magpie*.

But, as in his father's case, there was time enough to show that the success Prince Charles made of commanding his own ship epitomized everything that he had gained from his five years with the Navy. He had proved himself a natural leader of men and popular with all ranks in what is a very testing and intensely communal life. As always, his conception of duty and responsibility had been shown to be of the highest quality and his zany sense of humour never far below the surface.

The Prince had joined the Navy as an engaging and worthwhile young man. He left it, still young in years, his pleasing personality enhanced, and with the added self-confidence that goes with maturity. As Prince Philip said when the decision was made, 'The Royal Navy will provide the best training for the Prince of Wales.'

Above: The forecourt of Buckingham Palace, November 1975. Prince Philip and Prince Charles were about to leave for the Cenotaph and the moving ceremony that commemorates the dead of two world wars.

The Outdoor Life

Above: Charles has inherited his mother's understanding of horses, and has a strong rapport with his polo ponies.

Right: Like all people who lead their lives principally in the public eye, relaxation and exercise are as much a necessity for Prince Charles as a pleasure. Like his father before he gave up the game, Charles revels in the hard, hazardous and demanding sport that polo provides. But although now reckoned one of the top young players in England, he has too much concern for his ponies ever to show quite the same ruthless, match-winning determination on the polo field as Prince Philip.

Apparently there are a few sections of the public erroneously convinced that since the Prince of Wales left the Navy he has done little but play polo, squire attractive girls and generally live it up on the supposed manner of the idle rich. But they must concede that, even if what they suppose is true, Charles does at least play hard!

Like all the Royal Family, Prince Charles spends most of his life bang in the middle of the public eye, and that makes some form of relaxation as much a necessity as a pleasure. Physical fitness is another essential, and one the Prince always has in mind. By its nature, his job precludes dashing off for a game of cricket or football, even if he wished to. Golf is not a favourite pastime, and the only team game he plays, bar deck hockey for keeping fit on board ship, is polo.

When he was about 13 and his riding went into abeyance for a couple of years, Charles' interest veered towards other sports, amongst them the shooting that in season is part of the country life at Sandringham and Balmoral. He soon proved capable of contributing to the day's bag, and for some years the Prince has shared his father's reputation as a fine shot.

The interest Prince Charles began to take in polo when he was about 15 was scarcely surprising for one who aspired to emulate everything his father did and who was being brought up in a very horse-minded family.

Charles was taught the rudimentary strokes by Prince Philip, inside the indoor riding school at Windsor, astride a wooden 'horse' to avoid damaging the legs of a flesh and blood pony. He improved his riding technique hacking quietly about the park. By April 1964 the Prince and a friend of similar age, the son of the then Chairman of the Household Brigade Polo Club, were often to be found practising on the lawn at Windsor Castle. This was a place also favoured by Prince Philip for training and one where the Queen was always expected to forsake the role of mere spectator and busy herself heeling in the divots on the turf.

Before the end of the Easter holidays in 1964 Charles had been promoted to playing for his father's team in one or two 'friendlies' on the sacred turf of Smith's Lawn. Because of his youth and inexperience, his inclusion occasioned a few behind-the-scenes grumbles from the expert diehards expected to participate. But aided by two elderly but knowledgeable ponies, San Quinina, seconded from Prince Philip's string some while before, and Sombra, a present from Lord Cowdray, Charles showed promise and did not disgrace himself. Whether he would ever achieve quite the same hard riding mastery of a rough, tough game as Prince Philip—who, before a damaged wrist forced him to give up the game, was rated eighth out of the 400 or so players in the country—was a matter for the future.

Above and right: Prince Philip first caught the polo bug in Malta, and after that played whenever he could fit in a game, wherever he happened to be. Prince Charles is the same; this discussion of the last chukka is taking place during his 1978 tour of South America. But Windsor is where he first began to take an interest in polo on a personal basis, and that is scarcely surprising.

As young children Charles and Anne loved to accompany the Queen to Smith's Lawn, the polo ground in Windsor Park, where they could watch their father playing on most Sunday afternoons in the early part of the season. And since the Household Brigade Polo Club is situated just inside the royal mews, and the Club keep their ponies in the Top Court, much of the clatter of horses going out on exercise was and still remains connected with the game. The royal polo ponies are kept in 'Prince Philip's Yard', on the opposite side to the Household Brigade Club, and this was a favourite spot for the children to visit with their father. Polo was also in evidence nearer the Castle as Prince Philip often put in a spot of practice on the lawn, a custom later followed by Charles.

All in all, although Charles' interest in riding waned for a few years, it was almost inevitable that he should wish to play his father's sport, and he became thoroughly taken with the idea in 1964 when he was 15.

Since those early days, Prince Charles has played polo whenever he gets the chance. He played regularly for Cambridge, and although naval service obviously restricted his opportunities, he has seized the chance of a game wherever he could get it, in many countries including Ghana, Australia, South America and the United States.

The Prince now owns a modest string of ponies of his own—too modest according to some of the experts—and during the short polo season does his best to play at least once a week. Like Prince Philip, he finds the speed, necessary expertise and excessive exercise involved in this thrilling game exactly to his taste. According to his Australian coach, Prince Charles has more natural ability than his father, with almost faultless technique and great positional strength. With a handicap of three, he is now rated only two places behind Prince Philip. In 1977 he played for Young England against France, and captained the same team when they played America's under-25s. Some people, including his coach, think it will not be long before Prince Charles plays for, maybe captains, the English team; others maintain he will be handicapped by being insufficiently ruthless. Certainly his game lacks the aggression that made his father such a formidable opponent, but that has nothing to do with courage. The Prince is fearless, but it is not in his nature to ride his ponies as roughly as some players and in this respect the affectionate bond he develops with them could be more hindrance than help.

There will always be some to carp at this game that the Prince of Wales calls his 'one extravagance'. There are those who consider polo too risky a game for the heir to the throne. He has had falls and will probably have plenty more. A polo ball (which travels like a bullet and weighs roughly $4\frac{3}{4}$ oz) necessitated seven stitches in the royal chin. Now the hoof of his fallen pony has caused another facial scar. But to cavil at the danger of anything on which Prince Charles embarks, is to miss the point. The Royal Family themselves certainly appreciate that a spot of danger spices the sport, and if the Queen herself cannot participate she has an understanding and philosophical attitude towards her family's more hazardous enterprises. Take reasonable precautions, then forget or accept the potential dangers—that is the unfussing outlook of the Royal Family, and it makes for peace of mind.

When Princess Anne embarked on the chancy sport of eventing, the Queen and Prince Philip ensured she had a first-class trainer, and horses that if as inexperienced in the sport as their rider, had good jumping ability, and then encouraged their daughter in every way. It was a source of much justifiable pride that in 1971 the Princess became individual European Eventing Champion and in 1976 was a member of the British Olympic team. But it did entail accepting that the hazards increase the higher you go.

The Queen, however, takes the rational view that it is perfectly possible to fall out of bed and break a leg. And she was frankly amazed when someone expostulated about the risk of allowing Prince Charles to play polo the week before his investiture as Prince of Wales. She had never given it a thought.

Since riding started up again with the advent of polo, Prince Charles' horsemanship has expanded into other branches. He was soon sufficiently proficient to enjoy those rides out with Princess Anne, still fitted in whenever possible, where their shared liking for speed came to the fore. The Prince sometimes uses one of the Duke of Beaufort's horses to gain a grandstand view of the Badminton Horse Trials. Under rather different circumstances, when he represented the Queen in Nepal his mount was a gorgeously caparisoned elephant.

Charles has been cattle-droving in Australia and has tried his skill at the speedy art of 'cutting' cattle with a trained horse in Brisbane. Dressed in authentic cowboy rig, the Prince has ridden at the head of the famous Calgary Stampede parade. In June 1975, for the first time, he accompanied Prince Philip as escort to the Queen at the Trooping the Colour ceremony. On 7 June 1977, wearing the full dress uniform of Colonel-in-Chief of the Welsh Guards, the Prince of Wales mounted Centennial, the second of two black horses presented to the Queen by the Royal Canadian Mounted Police. His duty on the day of the Silver Jubilee thanksgiving service was to ride behind the fabulous gold state coach, drawn by six of the Windsor greys, conveying the Queen and Prince Philip to St Paul's Cathedral.

When he is available, Prince Charles enjoys Royal Ascot week, particularly the entertainments provided for the royal house party at Windsor Castle. Like his father and sister, he is by nature more of a participator than an onlooker. He appreciates watching racing to a degree, if not with quite the same enthusiasm as the Queen, and without the knowledgeable interest in thoroughbred blood lines that makes her one of the few experts in this intricate subject. What does appeal to him is taking part in the Royal Family's early-morning gallop up the Ascot course, an unofficial 'race' that was inaugurated by the Queen many years ago and is now usually won by Princess Anne.

This is not the only form of racing that attracts Prince Charles. Unlike his great-uncle, the former Prince of Wales, whose dashing exploits and numerous falls when point-to-pointing were of concern to King George V and public alike, Charles' creditable attempts early in 1980 at both flat racing and steeplechasing were generally applauded. By August he was the proud owner of his first 'chaser, the versatile 10 year old Allibar.

The Prince also likes to go fox-hunting occasionally. Again, unlike his great-uncle who fox-hunted without adverse comment, Charles is sometimes criti-

Below: Prince Charles has said of polo: 'I love the game, I love the ponies, I love the exercise. Its also the one team game I can play. It's also very convenient for me so long as I spend my weekends at Windsor.' Even so, not every game is trouble-free!

cized for doing so. Personally, he can see no harm in an ancient country sport that he enjoys, but is not one to go roughshod over people susceptibilities. One of the guidelines of his life is that 'You can't have everything you want'. If there were evidence of excessive and knowledgeable criticism of his hunting activities, then he would give the matter serious thought.

Given the time, it is very likely that the Prince would like to have a go at Princess Anne's sport of eventing. But that is something that does require many months of concentrated schooling of horse and rider. Prince Charles has therefore taken up the relatively new sport of competitive cross-country riding in teams, to which he was introduced by the Princess and Captain Phillips. This pastime is rapidly becoming very popular and provides enough galloping and thrills for anyone. The spills are also inevitable, as the Prince has discovered. His best 'scores' to date are two falls on one day, and on another a crash that damaged his nose.

So far, Charles has not embarked on his father's present pastime of competitive driving, a sport that includes taking a four-in-hand on a cross-country marathon. Again, since this is not something that can be undertaken without a great deal of practice, the problem is time. But Charles has done sufficient driving to be able to cope with a pair of horses as well as one in single harness. And his capabilities as a whip enable him to have the fun of taking part in a British Driving Society class, or to show the glories of Windsor Home Park to a friend, when driving one of Queen Victoria's favourite carriages, the ivory phaeton.

The Prince has come a long way from the slightly nervous boy rider who was usually outshone by his younger sister. Apart from enjoying horse-riding sports, Prince Charles, like the Queen, has a genuine affection for horses of whatever size or breeding, and he shares her liking for a really good gallop. But horses certainly do not form the limits of the Prince of Wales' recreations.

Fishing is a sport that definitely appeals to him. Prince Philip is a keen fisherman and has taught his son much of what he knows, and the Queen

Below and right: Various countries in the East claim the honour of having originated the game of polo, but the earliest references appear in what is now Iran, connected with Alexander the Great after his conquest of the country, and Darius, King of Persia. The game arrived in the West via English planters in Assam who played it on small country-bred ponies, and it was then taken up by the British Army in India. In 1869 some cavalry officers played a game of polo on Hounslow Heath, near London, and the game 'caught on' and quickly spread to much of the world, particularly to what was then the British Empire.

A good polo player is not necessarily a first-class horseman, but he must have a good 'eye for a ball', and since polo at top level is played at a speed of 20 to 30 m.p.h., cool judgement and courage are essential. In 1931, under the pseudonym 'Marco', Prince Charles' great-uncle, the late Lord Louis Mountbatten, wrote *An Introduction to Polo* that is still considered the best reference book available.

Above: Most forms of water sports figure in the Prince's pastimes, maybe because, as a strong swimmer, he is very much at home in the element. He seems to enjoy the new sport of windsurfing, despite frequently capsizing!

Right: At the helm of Prince Philip's Flying 15 *Coweslip* during Cowes Regatta Week. Charles has had some success in racing and enjoys sailing, but does not approach his father's youthful prowess and love of the sport.

Far right: In the warm sunshine at Deauville windsurfing proved even more enjoyable.

Previous pages: Comparative solitude is a rarity for the royal family, and something they all prize. Fishing is a sport that usually provides this valued seclusion and is one that, as with the Queen Mother and Prince Philip, particularly appeals to Prince Charles.

Mother originated Charles' interest in the art at which she is expert, but he was first taught fly fishing by a ghillie at Balmoral.

The Prince has sampled the exertions and excitements of deep-sea angling for tunny, swordfish and other big game fish. However, the more contemplative side of his nature is well suited to the quieter skills of fishing for salmon, or the even more delicate art of dry-fly fishing for trout. He has enjoyed trying his skill on the river Dee as the light fades on the hills around Balmoral, and on stretches of the Frome in Somerset. Since 1975 Iceland has occasionally provided a private and out-of-the-way fishing refuge, where Prince Charles can try his skill with a rod in the solitude that for him is as rare as it is treasured—and where the salmon fishing is superlative.

Several of Prince Charles' interests are bound up with his ability as a strong swimmer. He loves the water, both for exercise and relaxation, especially during some of the arduous tours on royal duty abroad, but he is too seldom able to have a quiet swim in peace. After the long flight to Rio de Janeiro for the start of the Prince's South American tour in 1978, there was a half day off to recover from jet lag, and the royal staff and journalists, who were all staying at the same hotel as the Prince, were able to combat the heat lazing beside a delectable swimming pool. But, despite an offer from the cameramen to 'hold their fire', Charles had to remain in the royal suite, to avoid the usual near-riot whenever he appears in public.

The Prince learned to appreciate Australia's wonderful beaches way back in 1964, and has been availing himself of their swimming facilities whenever possible each time he returns there. As president of the British Surfing Association he appreciates the exhilaration and difficulties of trying to ride Australia's vast curving breakers on a surfboard, but can seldom get down to the sea without the cameras and spectators that normally dog his heels. He has surfed in Sydney and Perth and swum in the bay at Melbourne but the hope of a quiet swim has usually been dashed within minutes by the arrival of several hundred onlookers eager to catch a glimpse of him.

It was Charles' strong swimming that made possible his adventure diving beneath the arctic ice. For the same reason, water-skiing, whether on the lake at Sunningdale Park, Windsor, or on a tropical sea beneath a tropical sun, is one of his favourite sports. Snorkelling is another. The Prince is president of the British Sub-Aqua Club and is now the gratified possessor of an international diving certificate. As president of the Mary Rose Trust, a society devoted to raising the 400 year old Tudor warship of that name, Charles has several times shown his skill as a deep-sea diver, going down 60 ft to the wreck.

Proficient swimming is also necessary for windsurfing, the relatively new sport which the Prince first tried out off the Isle of Wight in 1978. It requires good balance and strong arms and he was doing well until upended by the safety boat's bow-wave, as it tried to restrain the press boats chugging along behind. At Cowes in 1980 Prince Charles had a rival at the sport in Prince Edward.

Being a member of the replacement crew for a Gordonstoun ketch and five years with the Navy did not make the Prince an outstandingly good yachtsman. He is Commodore of the Royal Thames Yacht Club and was taught to sail by Prince Philip's old yachting friend, Uffa Fox. At the helm of his father's Flying 15, *Coweslip*, Charles has had successes at Cowes Week. But although he enjoys the sport he has never approached the delights and achievements of his father in the days when they were always a force to be reckoned with.

Prince Philip is expert at handling a boat, but winter sports are not his line, and he has little interest in the skiing to which his son would like to

be able to devote more time. Charles' first essay on skis was in Switzerland in 1963 when he was 15. Although, like most beginners, he spent as much time in the snow as on it, natural balance and a liking for speed inspired him with a taste for the sport. The following year Prince Philip took his two eldest children to stay with relatives in Liechtenstein where they were able to ski, and Prince Charles went back again in 1965. After a break of four years, Charles then had the chance of sampling the slightly different, and usually colder, version of skiing in which they indulge in Sweden. Naval service then put paid to this sport until a private visit to Isola in France in 1977 enabled the Prince to get down to some serious practice. In May 1978 he became Patron of the National Ski Federation.

There are not many outdoor sports that the Prince of Wales has not tried at some time or another, but he also has an intense interest in the things of the mind and the recharging of the spirit he gains from them. His youthful liking for drawing and painting, an echo of the pleasure his father obtains from putting brush to paper, was superseded by other occupations. But 20 or so years later it revived when the urge came to paint in water colours, an art form Prince Charles finds as rewarding as it is difficult.

Music is something he equates with physical exercise as a necessity of life. As a teenager, Princess Anne was a great pop fan, but had to 'encourage herself' to buy classical records. Charles has been passionately absorbed in classical music ever since his appreciation of it was first aroused, but as in

Left and below: Taught to handle a gun as soon as he was old enough, Charles was soon included in the shooting parties at Sandringham and Balmoral. He has developed into a fine shot, and is equally at home with a stationary target, as seen at Bisley in 1978, or at clay-pigeon shooting, when the marksman picks off saucer-shaped discs as they are projected into the air.

Above: After the cross-country at Cirencester in April 1978. For some years now Prince Charles' horsemanship has extended beyond the polo field. He has taken with enthusiasm to that cross between point-to-point racing and eventing where teams of four compete against each other across country. Given the time Charles might well have taken up Princess Anne's sport of eventing, but he compromises with this form of equestrianism that calls for a good horse, the ability to gallop and jump at speed, and plenty of 'nerve'. Occasional falls are an accepted ingredient of the sport.

Right: A rest between chukkas at Cowdray Park.

many things his tastes verge on the conservative. The works of Bach, Mozart, Beethoven and the operas of Verdi are the kinds of music from which Prince Charles believes he gains more the more he listens. Yet the chance hearing of a previously unfamiliar choral work by Berlioz moved him to tears. When in the school choir, he sang Benjamin Britten's *St Nicholas*, but he had to hear and rehearse it many times before he came to appreciate the work, and it was the same with Elgar's *Dream of Gerontius*. Once familiar, both works came to be loved, but the Prince has found few if any musical experiences to equal singing the Bach B Minor Mass with a big choir. The sense of participating in the creation of such music as well as listening to it, the great volume of voices, he found as exciting as it was emotionally satisfying.

But much as he used to love to make music, to do so with any success, whether with voice or musical instrument, requires the dedication and time for practice that the Prince just does not possess.

When he was at prep school he enjoyed playing the trumpet in the school orchestra, until the teacher's evident disenchantment with the sounds he was producing made him decide to give it up. At Gordonstoun, Prince Charles was inspired to learn the 'cello, after listening to the marvellously rich, deep notes of Jacqueline du Pré's instrument as she played in a concert at the Festival Hall. Although he insists his talent was exaggerated by others, the Prince played the 'cello fairly consistently when he was at Cambridge, and once he had the great experience of playing Beethoven's 5th Symphony with an orchestra. But he does not read music easily: once again it is the same story of insufficient time to fit in all the things he would like to do.

If Prince Charles no longer makes music, it certainly does not preclude him from listening to it. Even if his preference is for the classics and he makes little of modern music, his taste is catholic. He will never forget the inspirational music with which Yehudi Menuhin and his sister Hephzibah filled St George's Chapel, Windsor, during a concert celebrating the Prince's 21st birthday. But though the more unusual sounds sometimes heard on Top of the Pops strike no responding chord within him, he thinks the Beatles wrote super music and he enjoys anything with a good tune.

Good tunes usually have good rhythms, and the Prince was born with a compulsive sense of rhythm. Given the opportunity, he loves to dance. Maybe he has inherited the trait from his grandfather, King George VI, an excellent dancer who loved to lead the long snake of a conga down the corridors and through the state rooms at the Palace.

Prince Charles has displayed this gift on many occasions. Some of his favourite dances are the Scottish reels at which all the Royal Family are expert. He has danced to local rhythms with local beauties in Fiji. In the Bahamas in 1973 he relaxed from the formality of representing the Queen at the island's Independence celebrations by abandoning himself wholeheartedly to the pulsating beat of the merengue. Pictures taken at a reception in Rio de Janeiro during the South American tour of 1978 showed the Prince of Wales' unreserved and skilful interpretation of the intoxicating rhythms of a samba, in which he was partnered by an exotic-looking lady; next day the pictures were carried by newspapers all over the world. And while a formal dinner the Prince attended in Yugoslavia was not the time for him to join the exponents of various provincial dances being performed for the occasion, he could not stop his fingers from tapping out the beat.

Besides listening and dancing to music, Prince Charles supports another musical genre that he loves above all others. He is a Patron of Royal Opera. In 1977 he became President of the Friends of Covent Garden, a society that raises funds for various projects connected with the Royal Opera House, Covent Garden, and promotes opera and ballet through the money collected. The Prince, who always refuses to be a merely titular head, attends chairman's meetings, where his informal friendliness matches his helpful suggestions. Whenever possible, he attends the open rehearsals and gala performances and enjoys the special parties to which come all the great artistes who make 'The House' a place apart. An aspect of the Friends of Covent Garden that

Right: All the royal family have an affinity with dogs and horses and Prince Charles is no exception. His canine friend is obviously appreciative of the liquid refreshment offered from a well earned trophy, won at Cowdray Park, when the Prince, playing for the Guards Polo Club, beat the home team.

particularly appeals to him is the society's Junior Associates—lucky young people who can obtain cheap tickets in the amphitheatre as well as the older members' privileges.

Charles' fondness for dressing up and charades when he was young was encouraged as an antidote to shyness, and acting became a growing interest. At Cheam he took over the part of the hunchback Richard, Duke of Gloucester in Shakespeare's *Richard III*, playing it with 'competence and wit'. At Gordonstoun he progressed through Gilbert and Sullivan choruses and small parts in Shakespeare to a sensitive interpretation of the plum role of Macbeth.

Cambridge provided the Prince with good opportunities to satisfy his urge to be a comic actor. As a member of the Dryden Society he was able to give full rein to his talent for reproducing 'Goon' voices and to his liking for making a fool of himself on stage. At the same time he was educated into the slightly more sophisticated variations of university wit.

The success the Prince made of the parts he played in various sketches in the production called *Revu-lution* ensured his inclusion in *And Quiet Flows the Don*, another revue where his acting ability and humorous ad libbing were seen to advantage in 14 of the 40 sketches. And since university students are noted for basing their opinions of someone purely on his merit, their appreciation of the Prince of Wales as a genuinely funny man on stage was as gratifying to him as the good press notices.

Since those relatively carefree days, lack of time and opportunity have once more put paid to anything much in the way of acting on the stage. There are the impromptu occasions. There was that sketch when guest of honour at the Lords Taverners Ball, involving a pantomime horse and based on an incident when Prince Charles commandeered a pony to carry him to the wicket during a not overserious cricket match. Otherwise, except amongst friends and family, there is little outlet for an ability that brings enjoyment and satisfaction to its exponent and is an undoubted aid to him in public speaking and appearances on television.

But if this is another instance of actual participation having to cease, it has no effect on Prince Charles' enjoyment of the live theatre. Watching old films, usually after dinner at Balmoral and Sandringham, is something enjoyed by all the Royal Family, including Prince Charles, who aids his father with extra sound effects. But, unlike Princess Anne, the Prince has always been a patron of the live show, particularly if it is amusing and light-hearted and happens to feature the zany humour of the late Peter Sellers or of Harry Secombe. An impromptu visit to a theatre, sitting in the stalls with family and friends, is one instance of what the Prince of Wales considers an evening's good entertainment.

As for television, there is seldom an evening free for settling down to watch.

When there is, Prince Charles' predictable preference is for a good documentary, or something on the lines of Monty Python and The Goodies, or other material of the brilliantly absurd variety. His sense of humour is proverbial, but the things that strike him as funny are usually more visual than verbally subtle. Most of the Royal Family have a slightly 'Goonish' sense of humour, and the Prince was the Goons' number one fan. Long before he had the enjoyment of meeting Peter Sellers, Harry Secombe, Michael Bentine and Spike Milligan in the flesh, he was more than familiar with their radio scripts. In the encounter he was quite capable of exchanging banter for banter, and it was the apparent truth when he commented: 'Sparring with them was something I had wanted to do all my life'.

As a teenager, if there was no other form of transport, Princess Anne would use a bicycle for getting from A to B, rather than using her two feet. Prince Philip will walk if there is a definite purpose attached to the exercise. Each evening the Queen sets out for a walk, alone except for her dogs, for the break she needs in which to recharge the batteries of the mind. The Prince of Wales often walks because he likes it. He walked for four days on safari in Kenya, and reputedly outwalked the entire party. He walks on the Welsh hills in connection with his duties as Chairman of the Prince of Wales Committee, and among the heather on the hills surrounding Balmoral. According to occasion and place, he may see rhinoceros, or a herd of Welsh ponies or a golden eagle soaring splendidly above. But, as with everything Prince Charles does, at work or play, walking provides him with interest and pleasure because he has the benefit of a genuinely inquiring mind.

Above: Equally in need of a drink after strenuous exercise, Charles prefers taking his from a glass!

Left: Whenever his duties allow the Prince still joins other members of the royal family for the cross-country phase of the Badminton Horse Trials. On several occasions he has been there to cheer on Princess Anne and his brother-in-law Captain Mark Phillips, and finds the best method of seeing as many fences as possible is to borrow a horse from his host, the Duke of Beaufort. On this occasion the Prince was sporting a full naval beard, but this adornment was short-lived.

Around the World

Above: During what was a first trip to Africa for both of them, Prince Charles and Princess Anne had good opportunities in Kenya to see plenty of wild life. After his four-day safari in the northern frontier region, Charles said: 'That was something I really enjoyed. It was the best thing I've ever done, or one of the best....'

Right: Prince Charles is one of the most energetic and most travelled young men in Britain today. He considers that meeting all manner of people, talking to them and understanding their viewpoint and customs, are some of the most important facets of his job as Prince of Wales. In July 1977 on a return visit to Canada, he was made an honorary Indian chief, with the name of Red Crow.

Throughout her long reign, Queen Victoria went at intervals to Germany to see her relatives, and as she grew old she sometimes made private visits to the Continent for health reasons. But in the 64 years she was on the throne the Queen paid only one official visit: when she stayed in Paris in 1855 as the guest of the Emperor Napoleon III.

In this she was very unlike her great-great-granddaughter, Queen Elizabeth II, who has travelled overseas more frequently, on state and Commonwealth visits, than any other English monarch. And when Prince Charles decided that part of his work as heir apparent could be undertaken travelling overseas as an unofficial ambassador for Britain, he had the perfect example before him. He says that he learns much of his constitutional duties in the same way as a monkey learns, 'by watching his parents'.

Prince Charles began his journeyings in 1966, when he went with a school expedition from Timbertop to Papua New Guinea. It proved a fascinating introduction to the real tropics. And while there, he was installed, a little prematurely, as 'a successful fighting man of great courage', by the tribal chief of plumed warriors he met near Mount Lamington. Returning from Australia he sampled briefly the delights of Mexico, before spending three days in Jamaica attending the Commonwealth Games.

The year 1970 was a busy one for Charles. It began in February when he accompanied his father to the Council of Europe's European Conservation Conference. This is a subject Prince Philip has been concerned about for years, and in which his son also takes a very lively interest.

On 12 March, when the Prince accompanied the Queen, Prince Philip and Princess Anne to New Zealand and Australia, he had his first experience of the very full programme expected of the Royal Family on overseas tours. He also had a first taste of the royal 'walkabouts'. Although a little shy at first, he soon developed his father's easy approach with the immense crowds who hope at least to get a good look, if not to be one of the lucky few who actually manage to have a word.

On 8 April, having spent the day visiting an exhibition of the Institute of Applied Science, attending an assembly of school children, downing a buffet lunch with members of the Victorian Young Farmers' Association, and taking a look at an Institute of Environmental Studies, the Prince of Wales left his family in Australia and flew off to Japan.

He spent 12 hours at the fair grounds of Expo 70, visited 21 pavilions, and attended a reception for 350 people from 77 different nations. He also found time to sow the seeds of an industrial idea that resulted in the Japanese firm of Sony building a factory in the Rhondda Valley and employing local Welsh labour, thus helping to reduce unemployment in the area.

Above: Prince Charles during a military parade in Ghana in March 1977.

In July he was in Canada—another royal visit to well-loved territory, including a new trip to the frozen north, where furlined parkas were essential wear. There was a glimpse of Eskimo life in the tiny settlement of Inuvik and an abortive all-night vigil to see the midnight sun that declined to emerge from cloud. Then Prince Charles and Princess Anne flew to spend three days in Washington, as guests of President and Mrs Nixon at the White House.

In Washington there were the too pressing attentions of reporters and photographers, a picnic at Camp David and the inevitable romantic speculation about a match between the Prince and Tricia Nixon. And, as always, Prince Charles was his usual interested self, making his mark as much for his impressive knowledge of American history and politics when talking to Senators as for his humorous asides and what the American press called 'oomph!'

By early October the Prince was on a private visit to France. A week later he was in Fiji, garlanded with flowers, for the first—but certainly not the last—time representing the Queen on the occasion of a former colony celebrating its independence. Then on again, to spend a few days with the people who live on the atolls set amongst the lagoons of the Gilbert and Ellice Islands. An overnight

Above: Visits abroad often include long hours of watching displays and ceremonies. This one took place during Prince Charles' trip to Ghana.

stop at Acapulco in Mexico, two much appreciated days in Bermuda, three more equally appreciated days on Barbados—with an interlude for snorkelling—and home again. The year ended with attendance at General de Gaulle's funeral in Paris and then with a private visit to Germany.

Before Prince Charles joined the first ship of his naval career in November 1971 to start the voyaging on which royal duties could be combined with the requirements of service ones, he had an unforgettable fortnight in Kenya during the previous February. The Prince went with Princess Anne, who was to make a film for the BBC's *Blue Peter* programme. He went for his idea of a real holiday, to go off and be energetic and to see the few remaining wild places of the earth before they are built over. It was a first introduction to Africa and its vanishing wild life, and what the Prince and Princess saw entranced them.

While the Princess was working, Prince Charles went on a four-day walking safari in the northern frontier region, with his equerry and an experienced game ranger as companions. Camels carried the baggage, they slept in the open, and the only gun, to be used purely for protection, belonged to the ranger. They walked through the dry scrubland, partly by day, partly by moonlight. And

Above: Prince Charles in March 1978, with the Commander-in-Chief of the Venezuelan Army. As usual during his trips abroad the Prince saw and did as much as he could during his short stay in Venezuela, varying the territory visited between the centre of Caracas, the capital, where he could further his interest in industry, and the beauties of the National Park which as a dedicated conservationist he very much appreciated. Amongst other activities he called on the President and went round an aluminium plant.

Right: His travels often bring Prince Charles honorary titles and the robes of office that go with them. In Ghana he was invested as a Chief of the Bolga Tribe, and wore the ceremonial striped robes and cap.

they encountered only nomad tribesmen, and the animals the Prince had come to photograph: elephant, water buffalo, rhinoceros, and everywhere gazelle, all still plentiful owing to Kenya's far sighted policy of conservation. The lions came later when Prince Charles and Princess Anne spent three days together in the Masai Mara game reserve.

Before leaving the country there was an official visit to be made to the presidential residence 25 miles from Nairobi to have tea with President Jomo Kenyatta. Sitting there talking with the old leader and his wife, exchanging the presents courtesy demanded and watching tribal dancing, Prince Charles could not know that he would return twice to Kenya in the next eight years. He came in 1977 on a private visit to this land of wild life that captivates him, then less happily a year later to represent the Crown at the burial of President Kenyatta.

Until he left the Navy, with the rank of Lieutenant-Commander, the Prince spent most of his time at sea. During those years he took his special and very welcome brand of goodwill to a number of countries—in many cases on more than one occasion—and also carried out constitutional duties both abroad and at home. He was with the Queen and Prince Philip, and Princess Anne and Captain Phillips, in New Zealand early in 1974. Six months later he returned there to represent the Queen at the funeral of Mr Kirk, the Prime Minister. In 1972 he accompanied the Queen and Prince Philip during a state visit to France.

The Prince went to the Leeward Islands when serving in HMS *Minerva*, and while the ship was in the Caribbean, the people of the Bahamas gave the Prince a rapturous welcome when he arrived representing the Queen on the great occasion of the islands' independence. During those seafaring years, whether in an official or private capacity or merely stopping off for refuelling, Prince Charles saw something of 23 different countries and their peoples.

Since leaving the Navy he has stepped up his 'ambassadorial' role, with Silver Jubilee Year as the peak, and added a dozen or so more countries to his travels.

The Prince goes back to Australia—usually taking in New Zealand as well— whenever he can. An extended visit to the two countries, with which he feels his ties are especially close, was one of the highlights early in 1981.

One of his Silver Jubilee tours took him to West Africa. This was an exciting, brilliantly colourful experience with features such as when the entire Ashanti tribe gathered to do honour to the Queen's representative in Ghana, or, when on the Ivory Coast, thousands lined the route to Abidjan all shouting: 'Vive Prince Charles!' As of right he has worn the striped robes of an African tribal chief, and a magnificent feathered headdress as Red Crow, Honorary Chief of one of the Blackfoot Indian tribes in Alberta. He has sampled a soybean in a Brazilian field, sat in on a pow-pow in an Indian tepee, driven in a Canadian buggy, dined with Hollywood stars and ridden in San Francisco's famed cable car. He meets princes and presidents, high-powered business men, beautiful women and thousands of young people and children. Above all he meets people of all nationalities and religions and from all walks of life, and this is what he believes his travels are about.

The Prince's 12-day, 12-city tour of the United States in 1977 was rated an immensely popular success, if unrepeatedly strenuous. The 1978 South American trip took him to new and appreciated horizons. It provided too the opportunity to boost British trade and helped to clinch a big business deal in Brazil. In October that same year he went to Yugoslavia, following the invitation made by the late President Tito when in London the previous March.

It was Prince Charles' first visit to a Communist, albeit non-aligned country. From the moment he landed the Andover of the Queen's Flight, its red, white and blue paintwork glistening in the sunshine at Dubrovnic airport, it proved a little different to previous overseas commitments.

A small scout car bustled out to lead the plane taxiing to the edge of a red carpet where a naval bodyguard clicked to attention. A band gave a

Above: At the invitation of President Tito Prince Charles went to Yugoslavia, his first visit to a Communist country, in October 1978. During an intensive tour of part of the lovely Dalmatian coast he learned much of the country's history from the ancient buildings and monuments he was shown, and much of the sacrifices of more recent times from war memorials. Wearing naval uniform the Prince is seen leaving the tomb of the Unknown Warrior at Mt. Avala.

spirited rendering of both countries' national anthems and a Yugoslav television crew was supplementing the 37-strong British press party. The British Ambassador, members of the embassy and Sir Fitzroy Maclean, Yugoslavia's famous last war British hero now semi-resident there, were included in the welcoming group of VIPs. The airport had been closed to the public, there had been no pre-announcement of the date of the visit and security was tight. At times it was to become tighter, to the evident frustration of the British press.

The formalities observed, his hosts gave their visitor a first view of the lofty crenellated walls of Dubrovnic from a hillside where the road snakes high above the sea. The Prince was soon below, walking the clean traffic-free streets of this lovely town, the usual contingent of still and ciné camera operators retreating backwards as he advanced on the first of many scheduled tours of cultural and historic interest.

The Adriatic scenery and weather proved superb. In the towns the crowds grew a little larger. They were welcoming if puzzled about the Prince's exact identity. 'A British prince from England?' 'Queen Elizabeth's eldest son?' British and American tourists, there by chance, were ecstatic, touching him, patting him, thrusting over intervening bodies to grasp his hand. ('Good old Charlie!' 'I'm from London ...' '... from Boston', '... Leeds ...' 'I'm on holiday ...' '... a senior citizen ...') The British visitors in a hotel where the Prince stayed could not believe their luck.

Each day after an early breakfast, the official lunches and dinners were separated by long treks by car or plane, often still in the company of Yugoslav VIPs and their interpreters, to continue the dialogue. Each stop-off produced another ceremonial welcome, then more history and culture to assimilate.

The Prince was shown dimly lit churches, their domed roofs blackened with age, ancient buildings excavated from a rich past, museums filled with the relics of a brave history. He paused to glance up a narrow alley where house tops lean in almost to touch. 'You don't want to go up there when the washing's wet!' he joked. The press men jostled for position.

Inside the sites, pointing to this and that, asking numerous questions, he often betrayed a flattering knowledge of what he was being shown. He appeared

interested, he was genuinely interested. But even one whose pet subjects include history and anthropology who, aged 20, holidayed on a private archaeological dig in Jersey and concerns himself with the preservation of British cathedrals, can have a slight surfeit of historical remains. His expression was deadpan as he cut in on a lengthy discourse concerning Napoleon given by an elderly guide in so-called English, to suggest gently that his mentor would of course have been there in person to show Bonaparte around. The jest went over the old gentleman's head but the Prince's party appreciated it.

Prince Charles lunched with the late President Tito at Igalo, the 12th of the presidential residences. It is an enormous concrete half-palace, half-hospital with picture windows framing a spectacular drop to the sea below.

Like all the royal family, Prince Charles had a great admiration for Tito, both as resistance fighter and later, even in extreme old age as a powerful statesman and peacetime leader. Initially the conversation that day was restricted to formalities but, according to reports, over lunch the talk ranged wider. Wherever the Prince of Wales may be in a public capacity he has to carry a mental list of subjects taboo for political reasons. That must often prove frustrating for a man of lively opinions, but fortunately it still leaves him with a fund of 'safe' topics of world interest on which he holds informed and intelligent views.

A visit to the naval base at Split with lunch on board the corvette flagship of the Adriatic Fleet was one duty that took place in familiar surroundings. A tour of the Soko plane/helicopter factory was the highlight of the industrial objectives. Before the brief stay in Belgrade that terminated the tour the Prince flew to Mostar, ex-partisan country at the edge of the mountains. And if the Andovers of the Queen's Flight are not very speedy and, being turbo-props, can only achieve a height where turbulance makes drinking a cup of tea hazardous, they are as Prince Charles demonstrated, very handy for landing on small airstrips.

The party drove up from Mostar through the gorge of the green-tinted river Neretva, through country where the occasional pair-yoked oxen still pull timber down a mountain side on a sledge. The party abandoned their cars at the summit of the gorge and walked on up to the starkly simple partisan monument, fashioned in concrete and from afar reminiscent of a vast clenched

Above: During an official dinner in Belgrade, Prince Charles was entertained by dancers wearing the varying dress and demonstrating the different rhythms and steps of the various regions.

Right: Prince Charles visiting the Cheshire Regiment, of which he is the Colonel-in-Chief. He takes a keen interest in the British army and has also made sure that he understands the workings of NATO. He is being shown a 81 mm mortar.

fist. There, 1,100 m (3,600 ft) up and in a biting wind, Prince Charles listened to Sir Fitzroy Maclean's stirring story of the guerrillas who fought and won and died amongst that panorama of mountain and maquis.

As the years pass Prince Charles continues to shuttle to and fro around the world, adding to his knowledge of peoples and countries and the increasing complexity of universal problems. The majority of his tours are official, undertaken in his capacity of heir to the throne, but there are brief private interludes to countries of his choice. After Yugoslavia there was a day or two in Austria, before going on to Osnabruck and Sennelager, visiting parachute regiments in his capacity as Colonel-in-Chief. His journeyings in 1978 ended with a flight to Belgium to further his understanding of the workings of the EEC and specialized functions of NATO and SHAPE. That was followed by a three day holiday in Spain.

1979, as 1980 was to do, started with the opportunity for Charles to improve his skiing technique during a private visit to Zurich. Public duties then took him on an extensive tour of the East, including Hong Kong and Singapore. From there he went on to spend three weeks in Australia before snatching two days of privacy on the intriguingly named Lizard Island. Canada was next on the list, always another favourite port of call, followed by a snatched private return to Eleuthera, that exotic little island in the Bahamas that captured the Prince's imagination some years before.

The French Tours sur Marne in the same year produced one innovation. For the first time when abroad Prince Charles made use on his own of Britannia, employing the royal yacht's splendid facilities for reciprocal entertaining and then sailing home in her from Brest to Portsmouth.

Early in April 1980 the Prince was back again in Eleuthera for a couple of days. This time it was after a day and night in hospital suffering from heat exhaustion after playing polo in high and humid temperatures during a

private stop-off in Florida, following an exhausting tour. And it was typical of his impatience with what he construes as any personal physical weakness, that he then made an unscheduled return to Florida to prove his total recovery – and ability to play polo under the same conditions without ill effect.

The same month brought official attendance at a ceremony of much historical importance. That was when the Prince of Wales flew to Africa to be present at the Zimbabwe Independence celebrations, ceremonies that ended the years of UDI in Rhodesia and created hope for the country's future peace and prosperity under black rule.

Ten days later the Prince was in the Netherlands for a rather different but memorable occasion, the accession of Queen Beatrix after the abdication of her mother, Queen Juliana.

The year was to end with a 12-day visit to India, starting on the 24th November, followed by a week in Nepal. This was a tour of great importance previously postponed owing to the Indian elections, to which Prince Charles had been much looking forward. His appetite to see more of both countries had been whetted by the few days spent in each at the time of King Birenda's coronation in 1975. As the future British king and as a scholar in history the vast Indian continent, of which his great-great-great Grandmother Queen Victoria was proclaimed Empress in 1877, is of especial interest and significance. There was bound to be poignancy in going to a country so vitally

Above: The Prince of Wales represented the Queen at the ceremonies marking the independence of Zimbabwe. Here the Union Jack has been lowered for the last time at Government House. Standing next to the Prince is Lord Soames who acted as Governor during the period of transition to full majority rule. Lord Carrington, the British Foreign Secretary and his wife, Lady Carrington, are on the left.

Above: In 1975 Prince Charles represented the Queen at the independence celebrations of Papua New Guinea.

Right: A Prince of Wales fan-club with a difference! Some enthusiastic admirers of Prince Charles, whom he met in Abidjan, capital of the Ivory Coast.

Below: The Prince's sense of humour invokes a response wherever he goes, as here, sharing a joke with his guides before setting off on safari in Kenya.

connected with his late friend and mentor, Lord Louis, who as the last Viceroy helped end British rule in 1947 and created the partition of the country. But everywhere this was tempered by the high esteem in which the name of Mountbatten is held. On the purely sporting side, to be able to play polo in the land from which it was originally exported to Britain added zest to Charles' normal enjoyment of the game.

Earlier in 1980 a visit to Ottawa and British Columbia had been made largely in connection with the United World Colleges, a movement of which Prince Charles is President and one closely associated with his interest in youth and overseas travelling.

The Prince became President of the United World Colleges International Council in January 1978, when Lord Mountbatten stepped down as the founding president to become, until his assassination, the International Life Patron. But although few organizations could be more tailor made to the Prince of Wales' own outlook, he says it needed all Lord Louis' persuasive powers to make him take on the appointment, following on in such distinguished and experienced footsteps. Eventually his scruples were worn down, only to find he was not being left alone to get on with the job in quite the way he had visualized. He kept receiving little unsolicited directives and suggestions from the ex-President, and finally decided the best answer was to take a leaf out of 'Uncle Dickie's' own book. He therefore wrote to Lord Louis to the effect: 'You persuaded me to take this on, saying you were too old etc. etc., well, now please let me get on with it in my own way!'

Lord Mountbatten was delighted. It was exactly the attitude he had hoped for!

The UWC scheme now attracts students from more than 70 nations. There are three residential colleges: Atlantic College, set up at St Donat's castle, Wales, in 1962; the United College of South East Asia in Singapore; and the United World College of the Pacific, Canada's memorial to Lester Pearson,

Right: During his journeyings at home and abroad Prince Charles has sampled most forms of transport. This time in Alberta, escorted by a contingent of the famous 'Mounties', the Royal Canadian Mounted Police, his choice was a horse-drawn buggy.

Below: Prince Charles is twelve years older than his brother Prince Andrew, but now that Andrew has grown up the age gap has been bridged and they are excellent companions. At the famous Calgary stampede, acknowledged as the world's greatest rodeo, the brothers wore similar stetsons, the headgear usually presented to VIPs who attend the show. Prince Philip once caused a small furore by exclaiming: 'What, not another one!' when presented with what proved to be the last of several ceremonial cowboy hats. But he explained that he did not intend to be rude, merely that he felt 'Enough is enough!'

the country's former Prime Minister and Nobel Peace Prize winner. There is too an UWC multi-racial Associated School in Swaziland, in the heart of Southern Africa.

The essence of the scheme is to bring together articulate 16½ years old boys and girls, selected by scholarship alone for academic potential and personal qualities, for a two-year pre-university course. And it works. Mixed together, Jew with Arab, black with white, east with west, the students quickly come to see each other as individuals, in terms of common humanity instead of by race, creed, parental status or economic background.

It is an exciting enterprise based broadly on the philosophy of Kurt Hahn. Allied to a testing academic curriculum that fulfils university entry requirements in most countries of the world are his ideals of community service, and where possible, communal adventurous projects. At St Donat's, for instance, the students help with mountain rescue and have sole lifeboat responsibility for a 21-mile strip of the South Wales coast. Under hazardous conditions where team-work is essential they have saved 150 lives to date.

These are much the same tenets that through Gordonstoun were built into Prince Charles' own education. Combined with his deep concern with world peace and issues, his love of adventure and particular regard for young people, he is obviously cut out to be involved with just such a venture. As for the students, they know their President as a man who does not sit around surveying the scene but one who enjoys jumping out of aeroplanes or having a go at a Commando assault course. When he visits them at St Donat's he is liable to take out their latest Atlantic class lifeboat and coxswain it himself as a matter of course. One of Charles' strongest qualities is ease of communication whatever the age group and this, linked with his day-by-day interest in them and their activities, enables him to get straight through to the students without any hint of a barrier.

The Prince's qualifications for President do not however end there. He has

Below: Smoking the pipe of peace during a pow-wow with Indian chiefs of the Blackfoot tribe in Alberta, the Prince listened to their protest about their treatment by white Canadians, and hardship in the Indian reservations. He was able to tell them that the Canadian government were determined to find answers to the problems.

Right: The picture that was one of several of the same occasion circulating the world the morning after they were taken—Prince Charles in Rio de Janiero, demonstrating with an exotically costumed exponent of the art of Samba dancing, that he too possesses a compelling, inborn sense of rhythm.

Far right: One of the Prince of Wales' many important roles is as an unofficial 'trade ambassador' for Britain. In Brazil he was able to put over one of his 'back British business' campaigns as he toured the futuristic buildings of Brasilia, the capital.

proved well fitted to take the chair at meetings and help cope with the extensive business side. At his first meeting he was faced with representatives from 26 countries and observers from the Waterford/Kamhlaba School, Swaziland, the British Council, the British Government's Department of Education and other bodies, with the added strain of operating under coverage by television, film and radio. Most of those present were considerably older than the Prince and a few may well have been somewhat sceptical of the abilities of such a young man.

It must have been a daunting occasion, but the Prince of Wales took immediate command of the meeting, mastering his minutes, making statements with competence, and putting over his suggestions with becoming modesty. His idea that the UWC might contribute further to the solution of world problems by helping to tackle such pressing needs as global food shortages was unaminously approved. And he followed up with a resumé of conversations held with the President of Venezuela about founding an agriculturally orientated United World College in that country. No pie in the sky this, but a concrete vision now on its way to being realized.

Planting for posterity, one of the stated aims of the United World Colleges and other forward thinking associations, will always interest Prince Charles. The future, as well as the present, is his world too.

Ireland by the IRA a few hours after Lord Mountbatten was murdered. When his ship was stationed in the West Indies the Prince provided his regiments with a reciprocal report about his own life out there. As communications officer in the Pacific he set up an interservice communications exercise. And after listening to some of the complaints about language difficults from servicemen stationed in Germany, their Colonel-in-Chief compiled and sent them a light-hearted phrase book to assist in their amorous approaches.

Prince Charles is not included in the Civil List. As Duke of Cornwall he pays his way from half the income derived from the Duchy's 100,000 acres, situated mostly in South-West England and the Scilly Isles plus another 45 acres in London. The other half of the income is handed back to the State. Some additional, more curious benefits to which he is entitled even if he does not accept them, range from unclaimed wrecks on the Cornish coast to unclaimed money from Cornish inhabitants dying intestate.

Although an absentee landlord, Prince Charles has ensured that he remains a deeply involved and conscientious one. He has visited as much of the vast property as often as he can, meeting as many tenants as possible, and since his inheritance, has been actively engaged with the council that administers the estate. He has been endeavouring to find time from his other commitments to spend more in the West country. In 1980 when the Duchy of Cornwall purchased the Highgrove Estate as an addition to its land holdings in Gloucestershire, the possibility turned to fact. The estate will remain in the ownership of the Duchy, and Highgrove, the principal house, will be occupied by the Prince of Wales.

A certain amount of work, chiefly decorating and re-wiring was necessary, and during the autumn and following spring Prince Charles fitted in as many visits as his commitments would allow to organize the house for longterm occcupation.

For some years it was thought the Prince would make his home at Chevening House, a country mansion in Kent. The estate was left to the nation by the late Lord Stanhope for possible use by Britain's heir to the throne or other high-ranking public figure, or to revert to the National Trust. For various reasons Prince Charles decided to relinquish his claim, and when the opportunity arose his choice fell on Highgrove, a Georgian house in the Cotswolds previously owned by the Conservative MP, Mr Maurice Macmillan.

Right: For someone who includes acting amongst his interests, Prince Charles' Hollywood visit in 1977 must have been very enjoyable—especially when it included meeting such notables as (second from left) Lee Majors, Farrah Fawcett-Majors, and (right) Sophia Loren.

The property is close by the Badminton Estate, the home of the Duke of Beaufort a lifelong friend of the royal family and until lately the Master of Horse.

A big attraction to Prince Charles, essentially a countryman and brought up to appreciate the Queen and Prince Philip's active concern in the royal farms, is the 347 acre farm that goes with Highgrove. The land has always been of special interest, much of the Duchy of Cornwall's property consists of prosperous farmland, and now that he has his own acreage the Prince intends running it as a commercial enterprise. Future policy is most likely to be based on growing cereals and raising beef cattle.

Farming will therefore provide yet another angle to Charles' many sided private life. His public commitments range a little wider each year. They vary from the royal obligation to plant a commemorative tree to initiating discussions on matters of moment like national fuel and energy problems. World peace, world food shortages, the Commonwealth, human industrial relations and, increasingly, national morale and the malaise affecting industry, are some of the matters he makes his concern. On many he is required to speak and does so with skill, good sense and an appreciated leavening of wit. The number of times he speaks publicly in a year now surpasses even Prince Philip's exceptional average. And if the number of speeches obviously necessitate others coping with the research, the words and views expressed are the Prince's own.

Occasionally some feel his enthusiasm may over ride discretion. His criticism of management in February 1979, at a moment when the country was suffering from a rash of crippling strikes, incurred the censure of those who felt they knew more of the matter than one who had only studied it from 'the outside' for a few months. This is criticism Prince Charles both understands and concedes is justified to an extent. But he does make the equally valid point that he does not travel round the country and other parts of the world with his eyes shut or without listening to what experienced people have to say. And possibly that sometimes gives him the ability to see things from a broader point of view and so to pinpoint the 'sort of issues which need to be raised and discussed.'

In the autumn of 1978 the Prince embarked on an expanding programme, by special request not on a 'red carpet' basis, designed to show him more of government, unions, management and business at work.

He began with a day in Essex, visiting factories of the radio, radar and electronic capital goods industry on an ordinary working basis. This was followed up by attending a National Economic Development office working party meeting, concerning the goods sector of the same industries. Since then he has been to see something of the workings of Marconi Radar, Plessey, Cossor and Ferranti.

Other diverse engagements during that autumn included, as Master of the Bench, a Grand Day Dinner at Gray's Inn, a visit to the Warton Division of the British Aerospace Aircraft Group in Lancashire, and another to the offices of the now sadly defunct Evening News. He went round a biscuit factory, and an exhibition of Brazilian Art, presented awards to nurses at the Hospital for Sick Children and delivered the Hugh Anderson Memorial Lecture at the Union Society, Cambridge University. To wind up the year, amongst other commitments the Prince delivered the opening address to the Anglo American Conference on Alternative Energy Sources, visited Hyster Ltd.'s Plant at Strathclyde and the National Conference of the Industrial Society at the Institute of Electrical Engineers. 13 December found him presenting the Sports Personality of the Year trophy at the BBC Television Centre. The next day he was at the headquarters of NALGO (National and Local Government Officers Association). Early in 1979 he joined the board of the Commonwealth Development Association. His plans for 1980 included learning more about the workings of the Treasury and Home Office and other government departments.

A visit to Decca Radar in February of that year helped deepen his con-

Below: On that same trip the Prince met some of the cast of M.A.S.H., a favourite television programme: Alan Alda (left) Loretta Swit, Jamie Farr behind Loretta and Mike Farrell behind Farr.

Top: In recent years Prince Charles has begun to take a keen interest in British industry and he has applied himself to some of its problems. He is a firm believer in the importance of British inventiveness and feels that industry should make more effort to exploit and develop it. Here he is seen visiting the British Aerospace factory.

Above: The Prince leads an extremely busy life and he needs and enjoys his holidays like anyone else. On a skiing holiday to Klosters he briefly adopted a hilarious disguise.

siderable interest in the highly complicated electronics in which the country's future prosperity lies. In May, during a speech given at the Electronic Engineering Dinner, he commented on the sheer speed of development nowadays and voiced the hope that customers would not fail to appreciate the value of new inventions—something which he feels has happened too often in the past.

In his more recent speeches Prince Charles has frequently stressed his belief in the supreme importance of our manufacturing industries, the imperative need for technological change and the thinking that adopts it, and the urgency of encouraging more high calibre recruits from schools and universities to go into industry, particularly engineering.

He has said he sometimes feels that in educational establishments profit is perhaps looked on as almost a 'dirty word', that people appear to think being in production is less of a status occupation than being an academic or working in the strictly scientific research field. He champions British inventiveness, but deplores how seldom the good ideas actually get put into practice. And so, in these difficult times of the '80s, to help stimulate a much needed resurgence of industrial capacity and productivity in the country, the Prince of Wales created a new industrial award for innovation.

It takes the form of a competition for new ideas, open to anyone from individual inventors to small businesses or a group of sixth formers. But the idea alone is not sufficient to win the award: it has also to be backed and eventually produced as a commercial product.

To promote projects like this, and on other occasions sufficiently important, Prince Charles uses the impact of both radio and television. He is now such a professional, a fact in which he takes some justifiable pride, that he is known to the grateful camera crews as 'One Take Wales'. The medium is a hard taskmaster, and although the Prince is very good value, always a natural with something interesting and often amusing to say, inevitably some performances are better than others. It was disappointing that the BBC anthropological series *Face Values*, shown in 1978, based on Prince Charles' own good idea and in which he appeared, did not quite live up to expectations or do justice to the Prince's engaging television personality.

Although the Prince does not overdo his appearances on television, the media is yet another aspect that helps keep him abreast of life and work in the country at large. But if his pursuit of practical knowledge in as many fields as possible must make him the best informed heir to the throne in British history, he never neglects the purely constitutional side of his work.

The Queen has never forgotten the added stress and difficulties her father suffered on becoming King because George V had not allowed his son to see State papers. She has ensured that Prince Charles sees and has opportunities to study a very large selection of these important documents, and is able to discuss the relevant subjects with the ministers concerned. His constitutional duties include those of a Privy Counsellor and as a member of the House of Lords. He meets the world's rulers and other prominent people and enjoys discussions on the matters of the day with those truly 'in the know'.

All in all, the Prince of Wales may appear in many different lights to many different people but, if they delve, it would be difficult for anyone to suggest he is one of the underemployed.

Above: In January 1980 the Prince of Wales made a speech at a luncheon given by the British/Swiss Chamber of Commerce in Zurich. He sees his role as an 'Ambassador' for British business as an increasingly important one in a competitive world.

The Heir Apparent

Above and right: Prince Charles, conscientious, a romantic at heart, an upholder of virtues that some portions of society choose to consider old-fashioned, a man who can laugh at himself. With boyhood behind him, a Prince of Wales of more than ten years standing, Charles has successfully kept the delicate balance between being considered too trendy by the older generation, too stuffy by the young.

The human race likes to establish tidy milestones in life but tends to forget that these are arbitrary and based more on fancy than fact. Marriages are not necessarily more likely to totter at seven years, and at the official retiring age of 60 or 65 a person can be of more use to the world than at 21. On 13 November 1978 Prince Charles was neither more nor less mature, neither more nor less successful as heir to the throne than on the following day. The only difference was that on 14 November he was 30 years old.

Possibly press and public would not have set such store by the Prince reaching that stage in life had it not been for his unfortunate, if lighthearted, remark some years previously about 30 sounding like a good age for marriage. Not being infallible, he must occasionally regret some of the things he says in public. Maybe now and then his advisers have cause for regret as well. But few if any words spoken to date can have given Prince Charles more cause for lament than that casual comment made when 30 was still looking a comfortably long way ahead.

We live in an age of almost instant communication, and the popular demand to know public figures as people is constantly stimulated by the immediacy of television. The more people see of the Royal Family performing their public duties, the more they want to know of them in their private lives. Within reason, the Royal Family, and Prince Charles in particular, go along with an outlook that was unthought of in previous reigns. Even King George VI, better known and closer to the common man than any previous sovereign, held the view—understandable for one whose life is primarily public property—that the small remainder of it was exclusively his own affair.

But now the Palace, moving with the times, is very compliant about what is considered 'legitimate interest'—a point proved by the idea of making the television film *Royal Family*, and by the cooperation required of the Palace to ensure its outstanding success.

As a young man, Prince Charles was inclined to look on the advent of reporters and cameramen on all but public occasions as an intrusion to be resented. As he grew older he considered the problem more deeply, and having a sympathetic nature and being good at putting himself in other people's shoes, he recognized the demands the media puts on those who work for it. He never seeks press coverage but has to comply to a degree with the commonsense view that if no-one wished to write about him or take a photograph, there would be no point in being around. The heir to the throne has not only to do a worthwhile job, but in the eyes of the press has to be seen doing it.

One press problem with which Prince Charles had to cope was speculation about girlfriends and his eventual marriage. On these allied topics, which touch on matters normally very private to the two people concerned, the public

Previous pages: Prince Charles never lacked for attractive girl-friends, but the interest in his companions evinced by press and public alike did not make this side of his life very easy. On this occasion in June 1976 he was driving Davina Sheffield at a meet of the British Driving Society at Smith's Lawn.

Below: The visitor to Klosters, Switzerland, in January 1979, who suddenly discovered she was sharing a ski-hoist with the Prince of Wales! Skiing is rapidly becoming one of Charles' favourite sports.

interest is insatiable, and that does not make life any easier for someone who is by nature reserved.

The Prince may not be as conventionally handsome as some of his photographs suggest, but he is a very attractive man, with a sincere and friendly charm that appeals to everyone, young and old alike. Add to this his innate thought for others and the *joie de vivre* that makes him such good company, and it is scarcely surprising that he seldom lacked for an attractive girl companion who was not merely captivated by the glamour of his position.

Prior to his engagement, his choice was mostly for girls who, like Lady Diana, matched brains with looks and were interested in the same subjects and sports as himself. They also had to face up to the unremitting attentions of the media, as Lady Diana knows only too well.

Before her marriage, Princess Anne always gave thought to the publicity angle before accepting a private invitation. This was not on her own account,

but out of consideration for companions who might know nothing of the kind of publicity that royalty attracts and who would more often than not become unwittingly involved.

It has been said that with his romantic outlook Prince Charles falls in love easily, and also that premature publicity has killed off at least one romance that might have deepened into something more serious. It could not have been easy for any girl seen exchanging little more than six words with the Prince of Wales to know that some portion of the press may promptly begin summing up her chances of, and her qualifications for, one day becoming Queen Consort. Once or twice, sections of the press have had the Prince on the point of becoming officially engaged to someone he has scarcely met. Occasionally this was amusing, sometimes not, but, even if unconsciously, the effect must have been inhibiting for Charles. Probably there are some friendships that he has managed to keep to himself, but obviously he was in no hurry to rush into a marriage which would not meet his or the country's expectations.

It has been of the greatest public concern that the Prince of Wales should select his future Queen wisely, that she should be someone acceptable to his future subjects and worthy of the high office she will hold and the exacting role she will have to perform. There seems to be no reason to mistrust Prince Charles' judgement in this important matter, and every reason to believe he has chosen his bride with wisdom and foresight.

Ever since the Prince was of an age to be asked about a future bride he stressed that the subject was one to which he would give the most serious consideration possible. He stated that his head would not be entirely ruled by his heart, even though he hoped to be lucky enough to have both equally involved. His future wife would have to be very special and obviously Lady Diana Spencer is a very special person.

The moral pendulum has swung widely since those days of Edward VIII and Mrs Simpson, but the majority of British subjects still look to the monarchy to provide an anchor of behaviour in a bewilderingly shifting world. For the best example of a happy royal marriage on all counts, the Prince looks to that of his parents, whose private and—despite their different roles—public partnership has brought them great contentment and success through the years.

Above: Lady Diana Spencer, whose friendship with Charles caused an unprecedented furor in the press.

Below: The Prince and Lady Sarah Spencer, also a keen skiier, were at Cowdray Park one day in August 1977 when he was playing polo, and in between chukkas were sharing a joke with the wife of one of the opposing team's players.

Above: Prince Charles likes his friends to share the same interests as himself. In August 1979 he took Sabrina Guinness to a polo match in Cowdray Park.

Right: Charles has said: 'I love my home life. We happen to be a very close-knit family. I'm happier at home with the family than anywhere else ...' And this goes for members of the family outside the immediate home circle, like the Duchess of Kent, another of those with whom he can be completely at ease, and say what he wants without fear of having it recorded.

One marriage hurdle that produced a lot of gratuitous and diverse advice was the possibility of Prince Charles wishing to marry a Roman Catholic. The persistent rumour of his imminent engagement to Princess Marie-Astrid of Luxembourg, a staunch Catholic, appeared to be finally quashed by an unequivocal denial issued by the Palace Press Office at Prince Charles' instigation. But some of his other friends are Roman Catholics, and not long after the first official statement a member of Parliament made a politically inspired and distinctly impertinent speech about the hypothetically dire results to the monarchy if the heir to the throne should marry someone of the Church of Rome.

As the law stands, this would have been impossible unless Parliament had repealed or amended the 1689 Bill of Rights and the 1701 Act of Settlement, both designed to ensure a Protestant succession. And whether what might appear to the layman to be somewhat outdated laws should, or had been rescinded, is a matter for history. The alternative would have been for Prince Charles to renounce his rights to the throne, but that would have been very much out of character.

The Queen has brought up all her family as practising members of the Church of England. As Sovereign, she is Supreme Governor of the Church, and however difficult this title is to define, it is one to which the heir to the throne will one day accede. Prince Charles appears to have an open-minded approach to religion that includes the hope of more Church unity. His comments about the folly of Christians arguing about doctrinal matters that could only cause distress to many people were seen as reference to the late Pope's refusal of dispensation for a church wedding for Prince Michael of Kent. The words brought Charles public reproof from a Roman Catholic prelate and support from a Protestant one, and many thoughtful Christians felt that the Prince was expressing their own ideas on the matter.

In the meantime Prince Charles made it plain that he was well aware that the majority of people might not be prepared for him to marry a Roman Catholic, and that he would not clash with anything contrary to their feelings or beliefs.

For his own sake, and because of his duty to provide an heir, everyone must be delighted that the Prince of Wales has at last chosen a bride. As heir to the throne, his job is essentially a lonely one; by its nature, the job of a king is more so. In his abdication speech, the late Duke of Windsor was speaking from the heart when he said that the new King, George VI, had 'one matchless blessing' not bestowed on himself—'a happy home with his wife and children'.

The Royal Family is a very close-knit unit, possibly able really to relax only in each other's company, and they unmistakably enjoy being together. Prince Charles is aware that his sister is happily married and he sees Anne and her husband and their baby son established in their own beautiful home, Gatcombe Park. Their house, of much the same size as Highgrove, is only eight miles away. And since Prince Charles and his sister and her family enjoy each other's company immensely and share a mutual interest in riding activities, that obviously influenced his decision about where to live.

The Prince is himself a great family man and loves children. There is little doubt that in his own good time he will take his bride to Highgrove and that Lady Diana Spencer will be the 'someone special' who will give him the love, support and comfort, and the companionship for all their days, that he will need and deserve in the years to come.

Those years to come are another frequent source of public speculation. 'Will the Queen abdicate in favour of her son?' is a question that annually crops up. Prince Charles does not appear to think his mother will abdicate, nor as he has stated, does he favour the idea. And since 'abandon' and 'surrender' are two synonyms for 'abdicate', anyone who knows anything of Queen Elizabeth II's nature or moral code must realize how uncharacteristic such a course of action would appear to be. For it is the Queen's qualities of utter self-discipline and dedication, her total devotion to duty, that help to make her in her own way as great a monarch as Britain has ever had.

On the other hand, the Queen knows that a long wait in the wings, if treated as little more than a vacuum, could be disastrous. Each year Prince Charles' initiation into constitutional affairs is extended, and he undertakes more of the duties that help relieve the Queen of some of her burden. His programme of visiting institutions in the City is being stepped up yearly. He has no intention of sitting around as a king in waiting, and the tasks he envisages for himself are in addition to what he sees as his work as Prince of Wales, much of which is not particularly glamorous. The Palace has given up trying to list all the Prince of Wales' more mundane commitments. Predictably, the majority of the press, while acknowledging such work as praiseworthy, do not find it such good news value as the Prince's many friends, polo and adventurous undertakings. But since Charles' public image is founded largely on what the media choose to publicize, little wonder that he urges the press not to concentrate on the trivial. The job he does so well is not easy and would be envied

Below: Charles' role is not an easy one and few would envy it, but he is making an excellent job of being Prince of Wales, and his views on the monarchy bode well for the future. The Prince has said: 'I maintain that the greatest function of any monarchy is the human concern which its representatives have for people ...'

by few. He has every right to be taken seriously.

At times, the Prince has been dubbed 'too square'. Occasionally he is urged to wear something more contemporary than the neat suits he favours. But like his parents Prince Charles possesses great personal integrity and even in trifling matters would never agree to present himself as other than he is.

He has been called 'a glorious anachronism', and if that means he upholds some of the virtues now largely considered old-fashioned, then it is a good description of a future king. As for the future, the Prince accepts that modern youth is increasingly radical. He accepts there may be phases when there is less interest in having a monarchy, that by the time he inherits the throne political and social changes may have altered his role. But he believes the greatest function of a monarchy 'is the human concern its representatives have for people, especially in what is becoming an increasingly inhuman era'. He is a great champion of the individual, a decrier of 'the meaningless uniformity of mediocrity [that] seems to be stifling much of the world'.

A thinker, a man of action, the Prince does his best to do his duty as he sees it, but he is likeably human, possessing some of the idiosyncrasies common to the rest of us, and he does sometimes get tired, impatient, occasionally irritable. He lives under great pressure, and beneath the easy, relaxed manner he can sometimes be tense and unsure of himself. He shares the Royal Family's ability to accept, and then ignore, the despicable threats of assassination that, symptomatic of the age, increase in number yearly. Obviously the Prince falls in with any safety measures the police think necessary, and then carries on with the business in hand. But it must have been easier to dismiss such things as hoaxes before the kidnap attempt on Princess Anne and the murder of Lord Mountbatten. Prince Charles has himself had to grapple with a deranged man and cope with a bottle heaved through the window of his car. He also had a flight from the United States to Australia delayed by a bomb threat that fortunately did turn out to be a hoax. He has the endearing, and vital, ability to see the funny side of life, with a pronounced sense of the absurd. In fact, at times some of his practical jokes can seem a little laboured.

In his early thirties the Prince retains his boyish looks. He is friendly and courteous, with an attractive interest in other people's lives and points of view. It is impossible to imagine him being self-important, yet for all the informality there is an aura about him that makes it equally impossible to forget who he is.

Probably Prince Charles is the most qualified heir to the throne we have had in all our long history, and the future should prove that the British nation is fortunate to have such a man. With each year that passes he seems to epitomize increasingly the Gordonstoun motto: 'There is more in you'.

Left: Highgrove is in Gloucestershire, set in beautiful parkland and with its own 347 acre farm.

Our Future Queen

Above: Lady Diana Spencer and Prince Charles on the joyful occasion of their engagement.

Right: Lady Diana Spencer, whose family tree goes back to Charles II and who is 16th cousin, once removed, to Prince Charles.

The welcome announcement that the Prince of Wales and Lady Diana Spencer were to marry was made at 11.00 am, Tuesday 24 February 1981. This was the wonderful news for which so many people both in Britain, the Commonwealth and all over the world had been hoping, both for Prince Charles' personal happiness and for the future of the monarchy. Clearly everyone, including the couple's respective families, was delighted with his choice of bride.

Lady Diana is the youngest daughter of Earl Spencer, and 8th in line of a title created in 1765. Prince Charles has remarked that one advantage of marrying a princess or member of a royal family is that 'they do know what happens . . .' Though not herself of royal blood, Lady Diana is familiar with the conventions and restrictions that are an unavoidable part of royal life through her family's service to the Crown, both past and present. For some time her father was an equerry to King George VI and then later to the Queen, and her brother-in-law, Robert Fellows who is married to her second sister Jane, is the Queen's assistant private secretary.

Lady Diana was born on 1 July 1961 at Park House, which is no longer used by her family, close to the Sandringham Estate. She was educated principally at West Heath, Sevenoaks, a boarding school where good tuition is combined with instilling sound principles of character. Her parents were divorced in 1969 and since leaving school she has been working as an assistant at a London kindergarten, a job she clearly enjoys. She shared a London flat with friends but does not belong to the typical 'debutant scene' and, like Prince Charles, is basically a country-lover. The Prince has known her since she was a baby, although at 13 years his junior, until quite recently she remained the young schoolgirl sister in a family of friends.

This attractive girl combines vivacity with gentle charm and despite her youth has shown a courteous and dignified ability to withstand the sometimes unwelcome interest of the press. She shares Prince Charles' enthusiasm for skiing and swimming, and although she is at present no horsewoman she enjoys watching and applauding the Prince's varied horse enterprises. Without being especially academically minded her talents include an appreciation of music and marked artistic ability. One of their strongest bonds is a mutual love of children and home.

During the two years of their deepening friendship, Prince Charles has been able to realize his expressed hope that when he came to marry his choice would be someone with whom head and heart could be equally involved. In Lady Diana he has found the loved companion to share his days and duties, and one whose qualities promise those expected by the nation and Commonwealth in a future Queen.

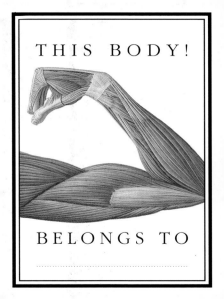

THIS BODY!

BELONGS TO

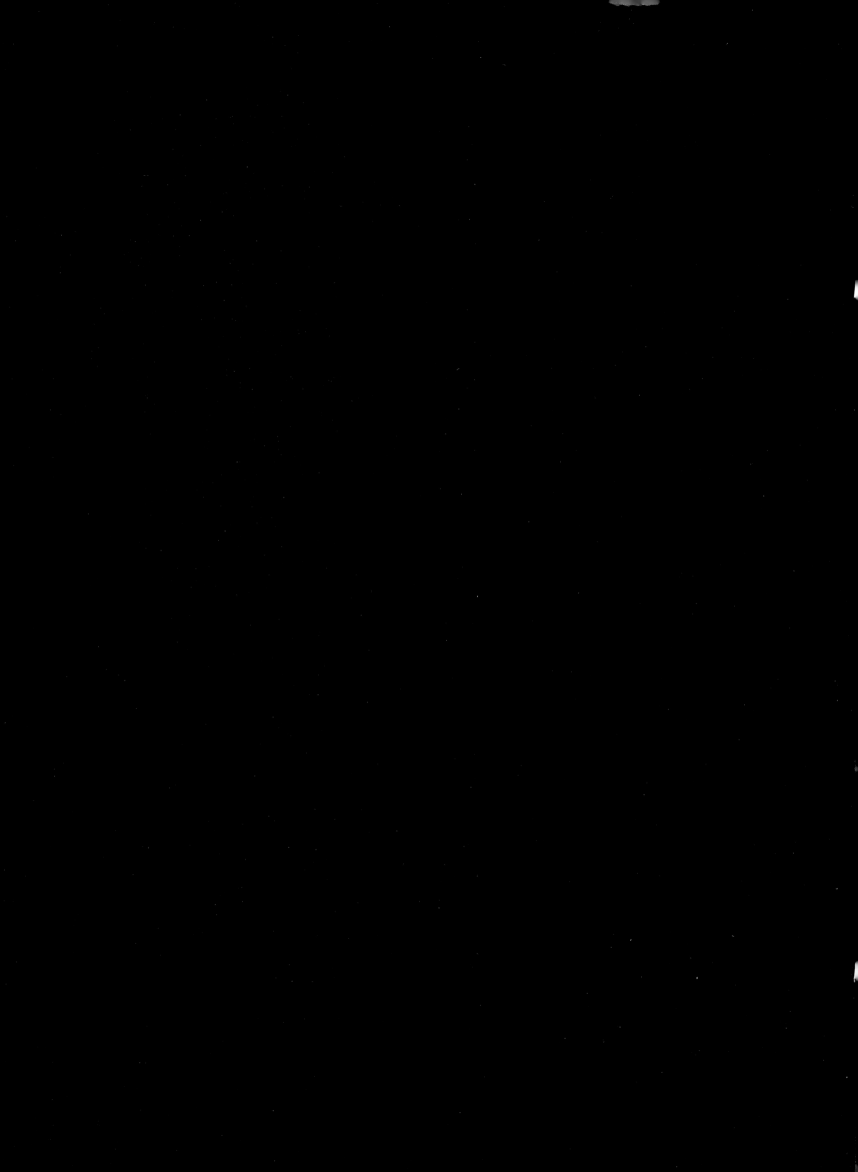

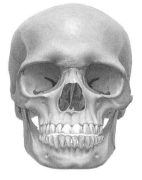

Your Body's Book of Records

Some Body!

Dr Pete Rowan

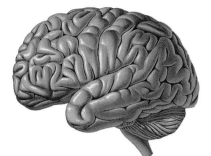

First published 1994

1 3 5 7 9 10 8 6 4 2

Text © Dr Pete Rowan 1994
Illustrations © John Temperton 1994
Dr Pete Rowan and John Temperton have asserted their right
under the Copyright, Designs and Patents Act, 1988
to be identified as the author and illustrator of this work.

First published in the United Kingdom in 1994 by
Riverswift
Random House, 20 Vauxhall Bridge Road, London SW1V 2SA

Random House Australia (Pty) Limited
20 Alfred Street, Milsons Point, Sydney,
New South Wales 2061, Australia

Random House New Zealand Limited
18 Poland Road, Glenfield,
Auckland 10, New Zealand

Random House South Africa (Pty) Limited
PO Box 337, Bergvlei, South Africa

Random House UK Limited Reg. No. 954009

Design and Art Direction by Peter Bennett

A CIP catalogue record for this book
is available from the British Library

ISBN 1 898304 51 3

Printed in Hong Kong

ACKNOWLEDGEMENTS
Dr Pete Rowan and John Temperton would like to thank the following for their
invaluable help and expertise in the preparation of this book: Dr Alec Black,
Dr Philip Evans, Dr Bridget Landon, Dr John Leslie , Dr Eamonn Maher,
Dr Tony Page, Dr John Pilling and Dr Alison Prior. The author would like to give
special thanks to two Hamiltons – the late Professor W.J. Hamilton who tried to
teach him anatomy and his son Dr David Hamilton who tries to follow the
tradition. Thanks also to The Guinness Book of Records.

Your Body's Book of Records

Some Body!

Dr Pete Rowan

with life-size illustrations
by John Temperton

Riverswift

London

Contents

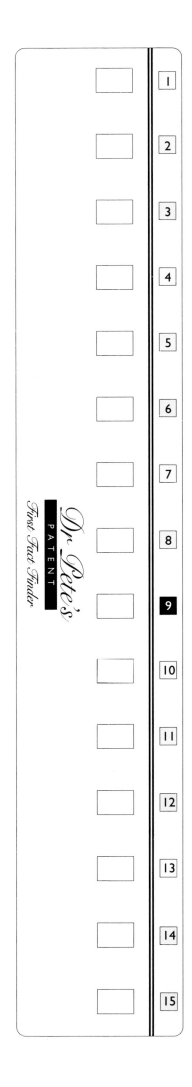

For Joanna May, who was this size • once

6 days	Embryo is implanted in womb
15 days	Mother misses first period
20 days	First signs of brain development
22 days	First heart beat
35-40 days	First bone ossifies
7th and 8th week	Embryo begins to look human. First signs of whether it is girl or boy
3rd month	First nails appear on the fingers
4th month	First hair appears
5th month	Mother feels first of baby's movements
6th month	Eyes first open. Eyelids and eyebrows obvious on face
7th month	Baby now "viable" for the first time – able to survive outside mother's uterus
8th month	Baby first hears and responds to mother's voice
9th month	
BIRTH	First breath
1st month	First smells mother. First wears clothes
6 weeks	First smile
12 weeks	First recognizes mother's face. First holds head up without wobbling. First grasps an object placed in hand
4th month	First laugh
5th month	First rolls over. First imitates sounds like a cough
6th month	First uses double-syllable sounds like "aghoo"

First Records

The first page of this book seems a good place to have a look at just when you first did or experienced things. They may be events that you will never do again – like developing a brain – or things that you do every day – like blinking. There was a first time for all of these.

You can also work out just when various parts of your body first appeared on this Earth. These are the cells, organs and tissues which, as you will find out later, hold many of the personal records in your body. And these are truly world records because, unless you are an identical twin, there is no one else like you. So your longest bone, biggest muscle and fastest nerve are all title-holders to be proud of! And the "smallest" and "shortest" records you have are just as interesting, and are all listed here in your own body record book. You are *Some Body!*

You can work out these vital facts about yourself by marking up a slip of paper as shown on the opposite page. It's based on a ruler and is very easy to copy. Mark the month of your birthday alongside the "9th month" and fill in the months of the year to either side of it. Then move your "ruler" across to the chart on this page and place your birthday month alongside "Birth". You can now read off the stages of development you were at on various dates. The timing of these events is more or less the same for all babies. So, if you were born on, say, 1 August, your heart began to beat around Christmas Day the year before, and you probably smiled about the time the new school year began. Using this system, my own daughter – born on 24 September – found out that her heart first began to beat around St Valentine's Day!

Some of the later stages in a baby's development are shown in the box. These dates or "milestones" after birth vary a lot between different individuals – a baby can walk any time between about 12 and 18 months of age – so don't worry if you don't fit into this plan exactly. Most parents can remember these milestones or have them in a "Baby Book", so ask about yours, and then record them on this page.

YOUR OWN FIRSTS
Write your own personal firsts here:
First smiled ....
First rolled over ....
First crawled ....
First walked ....
First word ....

5

The Cell

Cells are the units of living tissue, the building blocks of your body. Almost all living plants and animals are made of them. Your body has about 50,000 billion. The least number of cells a creature may have is one. Organisms with just one cell – bacteria for example – can be seen only with the aid of a microscope; but the huge collection of cells that makes up *you* can be seen in the mirror! Not all cells are the same. Like the bricks, tiles and panes of glass that go to make up a house, so the different cells – of bone, skin, blood and fat – go to make up your body. Most mammal cells are in the range of 5-50 microns (a micron is one millionth of a metre) in diameter. So whale cells, mouse cells and your cells are all more or less the same size. The actual number of cells is very different of course! An elephant has about 6.5 million billion while a shrew has 7 billion. Although the cells of the human body come in lots of different shapes and sizes and do a great many things for you, there is still a basic cell structure which is typical for all cells.

The cell's most menacing parts are the lysosomes. These are the secret police of the cell. They make chemicals which clear up any unwanted material, such as potentially harmful invaders like germs, or old and worn out parts of the cell.

The most productive parts of the cell are the ribosomes. They are the factories within the endoplasmic reticulum (industrial estate) and make protein. The proteins may be for internal use in the cell or, for proteins like hormones, for export.

The most abundant ingredient
is cytoplasm. About 70% of a typical cell is water – and most of this is in the cytoplasm. This clear, jelly-like solution is a complex substance containing many of the chemicals and proteins that the cell needs to stay alive. All the other parts of the cell float in the cytoplasm.

The busiest area of the cell
is the endoplasmic reticulum. It is like the industrial complex of a town. Within it are the "factories" – called ribosomes.

The greatest delivery service systems in the cell
are the vacuoles which move and transport material both within the cell and in and out of the cell.

The largest internal organ
is the liver. A group of cells working together is called a tissue. Different types of tissue group together in the body to form an organ. In the body different organs may be grouped together to form a system. For instance, the liver teams up with the stomach, intestines and pancreas to make the digestive system.

liver cell

liver tissue

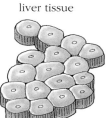

liver

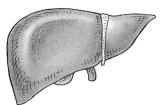

The most powerful places in the cell
are the mitochondria. These are the power stations of the cell. Cells which need lots of energy have lots of them. Heart muscle cells, which must keep the heart beating continuously, have more than ten times as many mitochondria as the muscle cells in your legs.

digestive organs

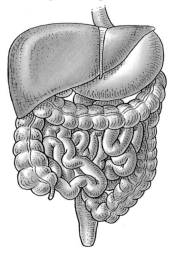

The most selective barrier
is the cell membrane. The cell membrane is a very thin layer of fat and protein, and it is one of the most selective barriers in the body. In other words, like the border guard of a country it's choosy about what it will and will not allow in and out. It allows food and oxygen into the cell, and waste products, like carbon dioxide, out.

The longest cell body
runs the length of your longest muscle, the sartorius, from your hip to your knee.

The largest storage depot
is the Golgi complex. Protein is stored here until the cell needs it.

Chromosomes, Genes and DNA

Male chromosomes

E very cell in your body bears your own personal body code. And unless you are an identical twin, no one else in the world has this unique code. The code itself is carried by 46 particles inside each cell nucleus. These particles are called chromosomes. They are usually shown like this. The 46 human chromosomes in the male cell and the female cell have been arranged in pairs. One of each pair has come from the mother and the other from the father. The male chromosomes are my own. All but one of the pairs look the same. This 23rd pair is made up of my two sex chromosomes. X is the "female" chromosome and Y the "male". All males have an XY pair. The Y is easy to spot because it's much smaller than an X. The X came from my mother, the Y from my father. The female chromosomes are my daughter's. Her sex chromosomes (again the 23rd pair) can be seen to be an XX pattern which all girls have. One of the Xs came from her mum and the other X from me. As they both look the same there's no way of telling which is which. You can think of each chromosome as being a large cookery book. Within these 23 "books" there are about 100,000 recipes – these are the genes. Each of your genes carries something that you have inherited from your parents. It may be anything from hair and eye colour to how tall you are. The words in the cookery book that make up the recipes are DNA (DeoxyriboNucleic Acid).

If the strips of DNA in a human cell could be unravelled they would be about 2 m long. Just as a greater number of chromosomes does not make for an increase in complexity of an animal, nor does an increase in DNA length make for more advanced creatures, unless the frog knows something about itself that we don't!

Longest DNA (unravelled)	
1. FROG	2.5 METRES
2. HUMAN	2.0 METRES
3. PIGEON	0.6 METRES
4. STARFISH	0.3 METRES

The most popular code in the history of the world
is DNA, the substance that stores your genetic code material in the nucleus of each cell. The plans for all living animals and plants are based on DNA. You may have more close relatives than you think – it has been said that the DNA in a chimpanzee cell differs from yours by less than 2%.

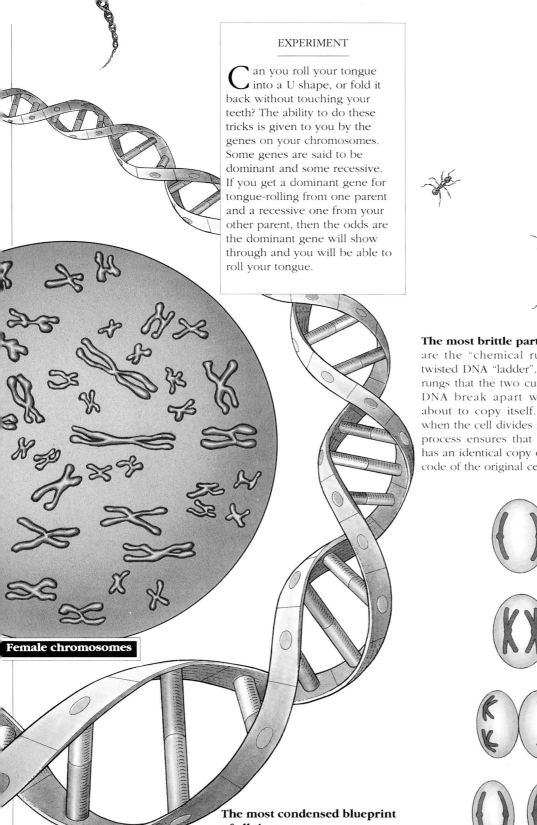

Can you roll your tongue into a U shape, or fold it back without touching your teeth? The ability to do these tricks is given to you by the genes on your chromosomes. Some genes are said to be dominant and some recessive. If you get a dominant gene for tongue-rolling from one parent and a recessive one from your other parent, then the odds are the dominant gene will show through and you will be able to roll your tongue.

Female chromosomes

The most condensed blueprint of all time
is DNA. Each of your cells contains about six millionths of a millionth of a gram of DNA. It's been worked out that the DNA of all the people born since Jesus Christ weighs little more than 1 g.

You might think that the more advanced animals – like us – would have the most chromosomes. This is not the case. The number of chromosomes a creature has came about by chance and doesn't mean very much at all.

MOST CHROMOSOMES TOP TEN		
1. FERN	1260	CHROMOSOMES
2. CHICKEN	78	CHROMOSOMES
3. SNAILS	54	CHROMOSOMES
4. HUMANS	46	CHROMOSOMES
5. MOUSE	40	CHROMOSOMES
6. CAT	38	CHROMOSOMES
7. FROG	26	CHROMOSOMES
8. HAMSTER	22	CHROMOSOMES
9. HONEY BEE	16	CHROMOSOMES
10. ANT	2	CHROMOSOMES

The most brittle parts of DNA
are the "chemical rungs" of the twisted DNA "ladder". It is at these rungs that the two curly strands of DNA break apart when DNA is about to copy itself. It does this when the cell divides into two. The process ensures that the new cell has an identical copy of the genetic code of the original cell.

The only sort of human cell without 46 chromosomes
is a female's egg and a male's sperm cell, both of which have only 23 chromosomes. The simple maths of 23+23 = 46 chromosomes = 1 individual person is all the maths you need to understand sex and reproduction! It's also the reason families look like one another.

Skin, Hair, Teeth and Nails

The largest organ of the body is your skin. It's a complex boundary between you and the outside world. It weighs about 4 kilos. Skin is the most versatile organ you have and it does a number of jobs. It protects your body from everyday wear and tear, as well as keeping out germs and the rays of the sun. It helps control body temperature. Sweating from the skin helps cool the body off when it gets hot. And in cold weather skin reduces heat loss by shunting the warm blood into deeper tissues away from the cold. The skin and the fat underneath also act as a blanket when the body is in a cold environment. Although most of your body's waste disposal is done by the two kidneys, the skin does get rid of some waste, such as ammonia, in the sweat. Skin is also involved in nutrition. When it is exposed to sunlight it can make vitamin D – important for healthy bones, skin and teeth. Finally, the skin contains the nerve endings for the sense of touch.

Hair, nails and teeth are forms of skin. They all contain a much harder kind of keratin (a sort of protein) than the softer keratin found in the outer layer of the skin.

Hair

Each hair grows from a root that is enclosed in a little pocket in the skin called a follicle. Each root has a small muscle attached to it. In cold weather these muscles pull the hairs upright in an effort to form a hairy coat and trap heat. In human skin – which isn't very hairy – this just gives a person "goose flesh".

The fastest hair growth
is on the scalp, where hair grows 0.33 mm a day, and in men's beards, where it grows 0.38 mm a day. The average scalp has 120,000 hairs, and the follicles have a three-part cycle – they grow, they wither, and then the hair falls out. The follicles then rest for about three to four months before starting to grow new hairs. Every day, about 30–60 hairs are lost from the scalp.

The most dense heads of hair belong to blondes.

The fastest-growing "organ" in the body
is the hair (even though the follicles have a rest period). Today you will grow in all about 25 metres of hair! Each hair grows about 12 cm a year, and one follicle will produce about 8 metres of hair in a lifetime.

The least number of hairs are found on the heads of people with red hair.

The slowest hair growth
is on the back, the arms and the legs.

The commonest hair colour in the world
is black.

Teeth

The teeth are used to chew food. The incisors cut up the food rather like scissors, gripping and tearing it. Further back in the mouth, the pre-molars and molars grind it up. Carnivores like wolves and lions have big canines because these teeth are especially good at tearing up meat. Herbivores like cows and rabbits have big molars because these teeth are better at grinding up vegetable matter. We have a mixture of these forms of teeth because we are omnivores – we eat all kinds of food, both plants and flesh.

The last permanent teeth to appear
are the wisdom teeth. These molars at the back of the mouth appear anywhere between 17 and 25 years of age.

The first permanent tooth to erupt
is the first molar, at around 70–72 months for girls, and 73–74 months for boys.

The parts of the body most likely to decay during life, but least likely to decay after death
are the teeth. The reason that they can survive so well after death is that then there is no food, acid or bacteria in the mouth to attack and dissolve the tooth enamel.

The hardest substance in the body
is tooth enamel. The thickest enamel is on the chewing parts of the tooth, where it is 1.5 mm thick.

The only part of the body which remains unchanged throughout life
is tooth enamel. So a person in their seventies with a full set of teeth has enamel in their mouth that was originally formed when they were in their mother's womb.

The first teeth to appear
are the 20 milk teeth. From the age of about six, they are gradually replaced by a set of 32 permanent teeth.

The last milk teeth to arrive
are the upper second molars, at 27 months.

The first milk teeth to fall out
are the incisors, at around the age of seven.

The first milk teeth to arrive
are the lower central incisors, at about 7–12 months.

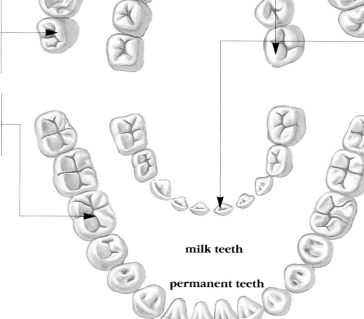

milk teeth

permanent teeth

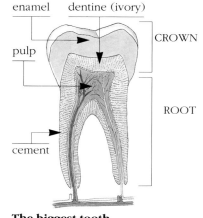

enamel   dentine (ivory)

pulp

cement

CROWN

ROOT

The biggest tooth
is the first upper molar.

NUMBER OF TEETH IN SOME ANIMALS	
SHARKS	UP TO 12,000
PIGS	44
HIPPOS	40
HEDGEHOGS	36
HUMANS	32
NARWAL	1

The Brain

Inside the bony projection of your skull is your brain – the greatest computer in the world. Made up of 85% water, weighing just 1400 g and looking like a pinky-grey, wrinkled blancmange, it's the control centre of your body. Some of this control you are conscious of – for example, when you turn the pages of this book. Other actions – like your breathing, digestion of food, and the beating of your heart – are under your brain's automatic control. Nerve cells take in and send out information from your senses, such as touch and taste, and the brain acts on this information when necessary.

The area of the brain with the most cell connections
is the cerebellum. Information about the body's movement and balance flow into it continually from the ears, the eyes and the muscles. The cerebellum uses this information to calculate the next body movement. Most of the control is done at a "subconscious" level and actions like walking downstairs or riding a bike are kept smooth and well balanced without you and your cerebral cortex having to "think" about which muscles to use next.

The smallest of the brain's chambers
is the fourth ventricle. Cerebrospinal fluid is made in the four ventricles and it circulates through them and out around the brain where it acts as a shock absorber. If it was surrounded by air, the brain would weigh about 1400 g but, floating in this fluid, it weighs only about 50 g. This makes the brain 97% lighter and prevents it collapsing under its own weight.

The most vital part of the entire brain

is the medulla. It is a control centre for blood pressure, heart rate and breathing. "Sudden signals" for swallowing, coughing, sneezing and vomiting can flash out from here.

The largest internal connection in the brain

is the corpus callosum. It links the two sides of the brain and keeps them working in unison.

The greatest relay station in the brain

is the thalamus. It is the gateway to the cerebral cortex. Through it travel nearly all the messages that the brain receives (though one exception is the sense of smell).

The brain's most alert lookout

is an area about the size of your little finger at the back of the medulla called the reticular formation (RF). It monitors the 100 million sensations arriving at the brain every second. RF filters out the hundred or so important sensations and sends them on to the cortex.

The most influential gland in the body

is the pituitary. Its front is an endocrine gland and the back part is a modified area of brain. This back part is connected with the hypothalamus, and together they co-ordinate hunger, thirst, temperature and sex drive.

13

The Brain in Action

The most influential piece of anatomy in the entire history of the world is the cerebral cortex – the grey outer layer of the cerebral hemispheres. This is where all our mental processing goes on – our ability to understand and appreciate the world around us, to communicate with others, and to decide on our actions. Events such as the building of the great pyramids (about 2900 BC), starting World War I (1914), travelling to the Moon for the first time (1969), and deciding to have a baby – including you and millions more children – all began with thoughts in the cerebral cortex. The power and size of this part of the brain set human beings apart from all other creatures on Earth. The total weight of any brain – yours isn't much heavier than a bag of sugar, while a blue whale's brain weighs nearly 7 kilos – is less significant than the size of this one particular brainy area – the cerebral cortex.

The most dominant hemisphere is the one which controls your use of language. In most people this is the left side. Most people with a dominant left hemisphere are right-handed. However, about one person in ten is left-handed with the dominant hemisphere on the right. The dominant hemisphere also controls reading, writing, skill with numbers and your ability to work things out. The non-dominant hemisphere is more involved with creative aspects such as art, music and the imagination.

EXPERIMENT

To use your dominant hemisphere, add 2 + 2 and write the answer down. To use your non-dominant hemisphere, listen to a favourite piece of music.

The largest groove in the cerebral cortex is called the lateral sulcus. The cortex of human beings is folded into many ridges and deep grooves. It is only 2–4 mm thick, but this folding triples the surface area to about 2200 sq cm. Two-thirds of this area is hidden within these grooves, known as sulci.

The most emotional part of the brain is an extensive area underneath the temporal lobe called the limbic system. It controls our feelings and passions. It has developed from a part of the brain once used for smell. This may be why smells are often said to be "good" or "bad" and give powerful reminders of feelings and experiences from the past.

The largest part of the brain is the cerebrum. It consists of two cerebral hemispheres. These make up about 83% of the brain's weight and are easily the most visible part of the brain when the skull is removed. They cover much of the rest of the brain in the same way as a mushroom cap covers its stalk.

14

The Spinal Cord

The nervous tissue of the spinal cord carries messages to and from the brain and the body. These travel in and out of the cord through 31 pairs of spinal nerves which leave the protection of the backbone through gaps in the vertebrae.

The most discreet and subtle part of the nervous system
is called the autonomic nervous system. The lower part of it is shown here. It automatically controls your heart rate, any involuntary muscle movement and any secreting glands. It's working now as you read this book, controlling actions like moving food through the bowel and changing the diameter of the pupil as light levels alter.

The largest parts of the spinal cord
(in cross section) are in the neck and lower back. The cord swells out in these regions because of the great sensory and motor activity of the arms and legs. The nerve root at the front carries impulses away from the brain, and the one at the back takes impulses into the brain.

front

The most prominent vertebra
is the 7th cervical shown here in cross section. You can feel your own very easily at the back of your neck, about where a shirt collar touches.

EVOLUTION

Fish in the sea, millions of years ago, were the first creatures to evolve a tube of nerves running along the body to its various parts. This evolved into the spinal cord.

The largest nerve in the body
is the sciatic nerve. It's a collection of fibres to the leg which leaves the lower part of the spinal cord. They join up to form this broad, flat nerve about 2 cm wide.

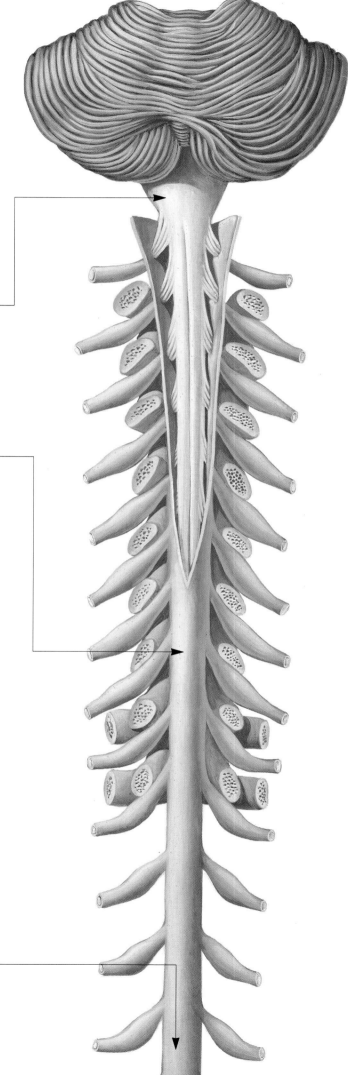

15

The Eye

The greatest input of information to your brain comes through your two eyes. Although it is only about the size of a postage stamp, the retina at the back of the eye is the largest collection of sense receptors anywhere in the body, providing 75% of all body sensation. The human eye can tell the difference between about 10 million different colours and grades of light – this can be compared to single-celled creatures which are able only to sense where light is coming from. It has also been calculated that the human eye could detect a match being struck 80 kilometres away on a moonlit night, and astronauts out in space have been able to see the waves made by ships at sea! In spite of all this, our eyes are still not as keen as those of many birds. An eagle's eye is larger than yours, and the owl – whose eyes take up one third of its head – can see a mouse moving 50 metres away by the light of a candle. The eye works continually to give the retina a clear, sharp image, and at the same time protects it from too much light.

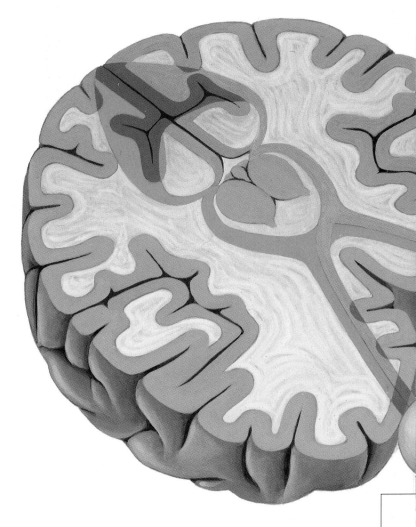

The most changeable part of the eye
is the pupil, the dark spot in the centre of the eye through which light enters. Depending on how much light there is, it can change size from 1mm in diameter (in bright light) to 8 mm (in low light).

The only part of the brain that we can see from the outside
is the retina – a screen made up of light-sensitive cells. It picks up new images at the rate of about 10 a second. An astronaut on the Moon can look at the Earth to see the continents and oceans, then down at his or her hand, then back to Earth again – and take in all these sights in less than one second.

The part of the eye with the most blood vessels
is a layer that lines the inside of the sclera, called the choroid. The choroid feeds the eye with nourishing blood, but it does more than just supply energy. It contains the pigment melanin which makes the inside of the eye darker, to give a better picture on the retina – rather like darkening a cinema so that you can see a better picture on the screen.

The greatest focusing arrangement in the body
is the lens of the eye. Small muscles can change its shape – making it fatter or thinner – so that, together with the cornea, it can focus an image on the retina.

The largest amount of information that the brain receives

comes from the optic nerve. Every second that your eyes are open, something like 1,000,000 new pieces of information about the world you see around you travel along the optic nerve to the brain.

X **O**

The most exposed part of the body's nervous system

is the eye when it is open. Set at the front of the the skull, the eyes are an extension of the brain, and need security. The eye sockets of the skull give a lot of protection. The eyebrows shade them from sunlight and help stop sweat trickling down from the forehead.

The toughest part of the eye

is the white outer covering called the sclera. If you could remove one of your eyes from its socket, you would see (with your other eye!) that it looked like a whitish tough bag about the size of a ping-pong ball. If you look in a mirror, you can see part of it as the "white" of your eye.

The most transparent part of the sclera

is the cornea. It is clear so that light can go through it. You can feel the bulge of your own cornea if you close your eye and gently press the eyelid.

The commonest cause of tears

from the lacrimal gland is emotion. Most spill on to the cheek. The rest drain down the duct at the inner corner of the eye.

The biggest and most mobile eyelid

is the upper one. The eyelids cover the eye with a blink every three to seven seconds. This wipes fluids across the eye and stops it drying out. These fluids are the salty anti-septic tears from the lacrimal glands, and the oil from the glands close to the eyelashes.

The most colourful muscle in the body

is the iris at the front of the eye. The pigment in it gives the eye its colour, which can be anything from light blue to dark brown. The iris can make the pupil bigger or smaller to control the amount of light entering the eye.

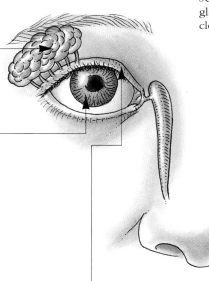

The most sensitive of the eye's defences

are the eyelashes. Each eye has 200 lashes, and when they are touched by even a puff of air they warn the eye to close for a moment.

The smallest land mammal in the world is the white-toothed pygmy shrew. At this size you need eyes on the side of your head!

The Ear

Your ear has two tasks – hearing and helping you to keep your balance. You hear when air particles vibrate and make waves of sound. These are gathered up by the trumpet of your ear and travel down the ear canal to hit the eardrum. The vibrations of the eardrum are passed along a system of tiny bones to the fluid-filled cochlea. Hair-like cells inside this coiled tube turn the vibrations into nerve messages that travel to the brain. The brain then analyses and makes sense of these "sound messages". On top of the cochlea are three small, curved, bony tubes set in different positions. One is upright, one is on its side and the third lies flat. When your head moves, a liquid in the tubes moves too, bending tiny hairs that stick out into the liquid, and sends signals to the brain to adjust your muscles and keep the body balanced.

The greatest sound amplification anywhere in the body
occurs when sound hits the tympanic membrane (eardrum). The three bones in the middle of the ear (known as the hammer, anvil and stirrup because of their shapes) are arranged like small levers, and can increase the original movement at the eardrum by as much as 22 times, making the sound "louder" if this is necessary.

The most forward part of the middle ear
is the cochlea.

The only part of the ear that we can see from the outside
is the pinna. This piece of cartilage, covered in skin, sticks out from the side of the head and helps to catch sound waves and channel them down to the eardrum 25 mm away.

Noise is measured in units called decibels (db).

Decibel Top Ten	
Softest Sound You Can Hear	10
A Whisper	20
Talking Normally	60
Heavy Traffic	80
Loud Shout	90
Rock Concert	100
Disco	110
Road Drill	115
World Record For Screaming	120
Gunshot	140

The only part of the body to produce wax
is the ear canal. Each canal has about 4,000 glands making wax to help keep this part of the ear clean. Any dirt sticks to the wax and in time works its way out of the ear.

The only outlet from the tympanic cavity
is the Eustachian tube which runs from the cavity to the back of the throat. Its job is to keep the air pressure the same on both sides of the eardrum.

The smallest muscle in the body
is the stapedius, which is less than 0.127 mm long. It and another tiny muscle can change the arrangement of the three hearing bones in 40 milliseconds and reduce excessive sound being transmitted to the brain. However, this reaction time is not fast enough to protect hearing receptors from sudden loud noises like gunshots.

Upper End Of Range Of Hearing	
Babies	30,000 vib per sec
Teenagers	20,000 vib per sec
Octogenarians	4,000 vib per sec

The Nose

As air is sucked in through your nostrils, it swirls about in the nasal cavity before passing back and down the windpipe. High up on each side of the nasal cavity is an area, about 2.5 centimetres square, where smells are sensed. This site has millions of nerve endings shaped like tiny bowling pins which can react to smelly particles in the air once they have dissolved in nasal mucus (the stuff that runs out of your nose when you have a cold). However, this area is not always in the best position to detect smell. Sometimes you have to take a good sniff to send the air swirling up to the roof of the nose before you can smell something properly. After the nose has detected a smell, messages are sent back to the brain with information to be analysed. Appetizing smells may make the body hungry, whilst unpleasant or irritating smells may trigger a defence mechanism, like sneezing, which blasts the smell out of the body. Most of us can tell the difference between about 4,000 smells. A well-trained nose, such as one belonging to an expert who smells and tastes wine for a living, may be able to appreciate up to 10,000!

AREA IN NOSE SENSITIVE TO SMELL	
SHARK	2230 SQ CM
SHEEP DOG	115 SQ CM
FOX	53 SQ CM
HUMAN	5 SQ CM

EVOLUTION

Smell has the most amazing power to bring back old memories and feelings. This is because our sense of smell has kept its links with that part of the brain that now deals with memory and feeling. This link goes back millions of years to the animals from which we have evolved. For these creatures, smell was a vital sense used to find food, in courtship, to recognize a mate and in bringing up offspring. These activities evoke powerful feelings.

The only nerve cells that we know are renewed throughout life
are the cells in the nose that detect smell. Each one lasts about 60 days before it is replaced.

The most primitive of the senses
is smell. It was probably the first of what are called the "distance" senses (the other two are sight and hearing) that animals developed millions of years ago.

The only part of your face that sticks out
is your nose. The nose performs two important jobs. Not only does it take in the air we breathe, but it also helps us to smell things. It's in the ideal place for smelling – perched just over the mouth where food enters the body.

The most acute sense of smell in the natural world
belongs to the male emperor moth. When the wind is in the right direction, it can smell a virgin female emperor moth 11 km away.

The most sensitive of the five senses
is smell, so many scientists believe. Within a second of sniffing, minute particles in the air have been recognized as "wet dog", "old books", "mown grass", "mouldy cheese" – or even a particular classroom or a best friend.

The Heart

Your heart is a cone-shaped organ about the size of your fist. This hollow, muscular pump sits between the two lungs slightly to the left of the centre of the chest. It is contained in a slippery, thin, tough, fibrous bag called the pericardium. The pericardium keeps the heart in its place, and between it and the heart is a layer of fluid which lubricates the outside of the heart as it pumps away. A wall (called a septum) divides the heart into a left side and a right side. Each side of the heart is divided into an upper chamber (atrium) and a lower chamber (ventricle). Four valves make sure that the blood can only travel in one direction around these chambers. The "lub-dub" sounds that doctors hear through their stethoscopes are the sounds of these valves shutting. The left side of the heart pumps bright red, oxygen-rich blood around the body. The right side receives the blood back – now a dark reddish-purple because oxygen has been removed from it on its journey – and pumps it back to the lungs for more oxygen. As this is happening, waste products from the cells – like carbon dioxide and water – are breathed out. The blood is bright red again now and it flows to the left side of the heart ready for another journey around the body. The blood leaves the heart in tubes (blood vessels) called arteries, and returns back to it in tubes called veins. It may take less than a minute for blood to circulate around your body, so each blood cell makes this return visit to the heart and lungs about a thousand times a day.

The first organ to receive oxygenated blood from the heart is the heart itself, down the coronary arteries.

ly artery that carries ʒenated blood ʋulmonary artery.

The most highly oxygenated blood in the body is the blood that is about to leave the left ventricle on its journey around the body.

The highest blood pressure within the heart is found in the left ventricle. This isn't surprising, since the left ventricle is responsible for pumping arterial blood around the body.

The strongest and most powerful part of the heart is the left ventricle. Its muscular wall is three times the thickness of the right ventricle. You can feel your left ventricle easily. Press your fingers just below your left nipple and you'll feel the tip of it beating.

rgest artery ʌorta, which is 3 cm across at ɪnt where it leaves the heart ∍ oxygenated blood around ly.

HUMAN HEARTBEATS IN A LIFETIME

ONE HOUR	4,200
ONE DAY	100,800
ONE WEEK	705,000
A LIFETIME	2,500,000,000

MAMMAL HEART RATES TOP FIVE

1. MOUSE	500
2. RABBIT	200
3. HUMAN	70
4. OX	25
5. ELEPHANT	20

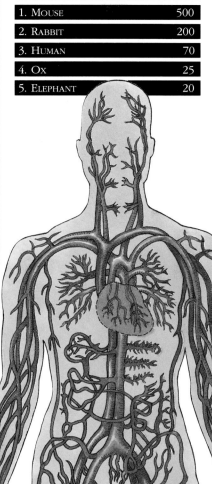

Your first heartbeat

happened in the womb during the fourth week of pregnancy when you were this size. It will continue beating until the day that you die.

The slowest heart rates seen in the normal body

are found in the very fit. Four healthy, super-fit Belgian cyclists had their heart rates measured at below 30 beats a minute when they were asleep. This is because, in fit people, the heart becomes very efficient at pumping blood – even during exercise it may only have to raise its rate to perhaps 140 beats per minute.

The largest heart

ever found belonged to a blue whale. It weighed 698.5 kilos – and was about the same size as an average car.

The slowest bloodflow

in the body is in the capillaries where red cells shuffle along in single file at only about 0.5 mm per second. It has been estimated that if one capillary leaked blood into a cup it would take 100 years to fill it.

The fastest heart rates seen in the normal body

come when young people take violent exercise, when the rate may go over 200 beats per minute. The average adult resting heart rate is 65-70 beats per minute. During exercise the cardiac output can increase from under 6 to more than 30 litres per minute.

Discovery of the circulation

In 1616 William Harvey told a stunned audience at the Royal College of Physicians in London that he believed blood circulated around the human body. For over a thousand years until this moment, it had been believed that blood ebbed and flowed like the tides of the the sea. Harvey argued that as thousands of litres of blood passed through the heart every hour this blood must be circulating. He also showed that blood in veins always flowed towards the heart.

The one thing Harvey could not explain was how the blood got from the arteries to the veins. It was left to Marcello Malpighi (1628-94), an Italian who was an expert on anatomy and also a pioneer in the use of the microscope. He saw the smallest of blood vessels – capillaries which have a diameter of about 0.01 mm, that's 50 times smaller than a human hair – in the foot of the frog and the missing link in the understanding of the circulation was made.

The smallest blood vessels in the body

are the capillaries. These vessels are the link between the arterial and venous systems. They have a diameter of around 0.01 mm so it's not possible to see just one without some form of magnification. There are around 60,000 miles or 96,000 km of blood vessels in the human body and most of these are capillaries. This is the part of the circulation where oxygen is supplied to the individual cells and waste is removed.

Blood

This is a picture of a smear of blood magnified 15,000 times. There are two main parts to blood. The first part is the fluid plasma, and the second part is the different cells which float around in it. You can see the red cells, the white cells and the platelets. Blood cells are made in the bone marrow. Blood is the great transport system of the body. Food that has been digested and absorbed from the intestines, and oxygen from the lungs are taken to individual cells to be converted into energy. Waste is taken away from the same cells and carried to the lungs to be breathed out (carbon dioxide) or to the kidneys to be passed out in the urine (urea). Blood also carries chemical messengers, called hormones, from the brain to the glands they affect in other parts of the body. Much of the body's defence system is carried by the blood too. Last but not least, blood also helps to regulate your temperature as it circulates, taking heat from the centre of your body to the extremities of your hands and feet.

The most abundant ingredient of blood
is water. Blood is 90% water. Along with salts, acids and proteins that are important for blood clotting this water forms the fluid part – the plasma.

EXPERIMENT

The only place you can acually see blood in the healthy body is in the retina at the back of the eye. You often see this in photographs when the flash light bounces back from the eye of the subject and is recorded on the film.
You can hear your own blood flowing by putting something like a shell or a cup to your ear. The sound similar to the sound of the sea is blood moving through the veins in your head. The shell is acting like an echo chamber and cuts out other noises.

The cell with the longest memory
is the lymphocyte. Successive generations of lymphocytes never forget an enemy. For example, once a measles virus has introduced itself to the lymphocytes in the first years of life, these stalwarts of the immune system will still be ready to recognize and destroy the measles virus 70 years later.

The smallest blood cells
are the lymphocytes (9-15 microns). They are an important part of the white blood cell system and the body's defences. They are made both in bone marrow and in lymphatic tissue.

The largest blood cell
is a white cell called a monocyte (15-20 microns). Monocytes can move quickly to gobble up germs which may try to enter your body. All your white blood cells are part of your body's defence system.

The most abundant cell in the body

is the red cell. You have about 30,000 billion of them. Oxygen is carried around the body in red cells. Red cells live about 120 days and then die. They are replaced at the rate of about two million every second! There are five million red cells in one pin prick of blood compared with 250,000 platelets and only 9,000 white cells.

The commonest white cell

is the neutrophil. Neutrophils make up about 65% of all the white cells, and they're made in the bone marrow. There are rarer types of white cells called basophils and eosinophils. No one knows exactly what they do.

The smallest visible particles in blood

are the platelets. They are also perhaps the stickiest! They float around and help the blood to clot when you cut yourself. Once a hole is made in a blood vessel the platelets quickly gather at the site, stick to it, and seal the breach. They are made from small parts of huge cells called megakaryocytes in the bone marrow.

The greatest trapper of blood cells

is the mesh of fibrin threads which forms when you cut yourself. These strands trap the cells, so sealing the hole until it heals up.

The rarest blood group

is AB. Less than 10% of the population have this blood group.

The commonest blood group

is group O. About 46% of the population have this type of blood.

Blood groups

Humans can be divided into four blood groups depending on the presence or absence of substances called A, B and O in their red blood cells.

The Lungs

Respiration is the process of taking in oxygen and giving out carbon dioxide. In land animals like us, this is done by breathing. When the large, flat muscle under the lungs – the diaphragm – moves down, air is drawn down the windpipe and into the two lungs. When the diaphragm relaxes and moves up, the air in your lungs is squeezed out. Put your hands on your chest and feel the lungs fill with air as you breathe in. Oxygen is needed in every cell for the process of releasing the energy in the food you've eaten. The oxygen travels from the lungs to these cells in the circulating blood. The waste products of respiration, such as carbon dioxide, are discharged from the blood into the air that is to be breathed out.

When you breathe out, air passes between the two vocal cords. Muscles in your larynx (your "voice box") can alter the length of these cords vibrating in the moving air, and this provides a change in the sound coming out. Generally, the tenser the cords the faster they vibrate and the higher the sound produced. There is a lot more to speaking than just changing the shape of the vocal cords. It takes several years for a child to learn how to juggle the movements of lips, tongue and jaw to turn the sounds into speech.

The vocal cords

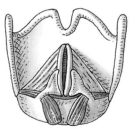

Highest-pitched sounds

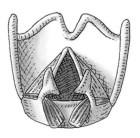

Lowest-pitched sounds

The widest part of the respiratory system
is the trachea (windpipe). Like the "trunk" of a tree, this branches into the left and right main bronchi. Lower down, the airways divide into much smaller air passages called bronchioles. These are the "twigs" on the tree.

The largest lung
is the one on the right side of the body. It has three sections – these are usually called lobes. The left lung has two lobes.

The Airways

There is a system of airways connecting your nose to the top of the windpipe at the back of the throat. The caves and tunnels of the upper airways are lined with cells that have tiny hairs called cilia sticking out of them. These cells produce a sticky liquid called mucus, which moistens and warms the air as it is breathed in. This gives the delicate lungs important protection from very cold, dry air which could damage lung tissue.

The loudest noise that your body can make
is a scream. The world record for screaming is 128 decibels, with shouting at 119 decibels. Both these noises – as well as your speech – come from your larynx.

The largest body sinus (hollow structure within the skull)
is the maxillary sinus. It lies under the cheek and occupies most of the area between the roof of the mouth and the floor of eye socket. The sinuses lighten the skull, give tone to the voice, and help warm up air as it passes by on the way to the lungs.

The fastest way air leaves the airways
is when you sneeze. In a sneeze, air can reach hurricane speeds of 160 kph! Usually the mucus and cilia waft particles of dust or pollen away from the lungs and out of the nose. If too much dust or pollen is breathed in, this system is overwhelmed and your body may need to sneeze to clear the airway.

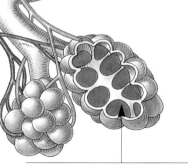

EXPERIMENT

You only talk when you are breathing out. Try speaking while you are breathing in. Some words you use your tongue to form (e.g. "Dad") and some your lips (e.g. "Mum"). You can prove this by trying to say "Mum" without moving your lips, or "Dad" without moving your tongue.

The smallest airways in your lungs
are the tiny tubes at the end of the bronchial tree. This is the part of the system that is furthest from your mouth. These tubes end in bunches of air sacs called alveoli. Each sac is surrounded by blood vessels called capillaries. The walls of both the air sacs and the capillaries are so thin – the space between the air and blood is around 0.0002 mm – that oxygen from breathed-in air easily passes into the blood.

The only organ in your body light enough to float on water
is your lungs.

The largest pump in the body
is the system of the lungs and the the muscles that move air in and out.

The Body's Defences

Your body is protected by an amazing set of defences – rather like those of a medieval castle. The outer "wall" is your skin, closely backed up by the filters, hair traps and membranes that guard entrances like your ears, eyes and nostrils. The next line of defence is inside your body, and is provided by the saliva in your mouth, the salty tears in your eyes, and the strong acid in your stomach. Coughing, sneezing and vomiting can all be used to expel unwanted invaders. But when a thorn penetrates the skin, or when a cold virus is breathed in through the nose, then the army of your immune system is there to stamp out the trouble quickly.

The immune system works in two ways. It has white cells which can gobble up germs, and it can make antibodies which can be fired like missiles at invaders. The immune system is linked together by the circulation of a clear fluid called lymph, which travels slowly around your body alongside the blood vessels. Most of your blood leaves the heart through the arteries, and returns to it in the veins. However, some fluid from the blood leaks out into the lymphatic vessels to join the lymph (it is eventually returned to the blood near the heart). As the lymph flows back towards the heart, it passes through areas called lymph nodes. These nodes act like filters. White cells within them are ready and waiting to destroy invaders either by gobbling them up, or by forming antibodies against them. Because lymphatic vessels pick up lymph from nearly all body tissue, the immune cells in the lymph nodes are in the ideal position to meet problems. Unfortunately, the immune system can only give you instant protection from an invader it has met before. It will take several days to react to a new invader.

The first part of the lymphatic system to appear in a developing baby
is the thymus. The thymus prepares certain lymphocytes so that they are ready to attack specific invaders once the lymphocytes arrive in the lymph nodes.

The most common lymphatic formations
are the lymph nodes. There are hundreds of these spread around the body, each one about the size of a small kidney bean. They tend to be found in groups near veins, and large clusters can sometimes be felt in the groin, under the arm and in the lower neck.

The most important cells in the immune system
are the lymphocytes and the macrophages. The macrophages lurk in the lymph nodes and can engulf and destroy any unwanted matter arriving through the lymphatic system. The lymphocytes are found almost everywhere in the body, but are most concentrated in the spleen, lymph nodes and the thymus. They are made in the bone marrow and in the thymus. It is the lymphocytes from the marrow which make antibodies.

The best-placed defences against invaders from the intestines
are the Peyer's patches – areas of lymphoid tissue strategically placed to stop invasions across the intestinal wall.

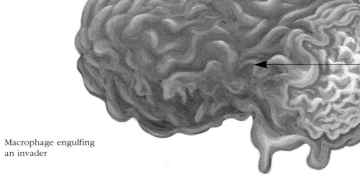

Macrophage engulfing an invader

The only part of the lymphatic system that you can see

are your two tonsils. Open your mouth and look at them, standing guard like two round, fat soldiers on either side of the back of your throat.

The largest duct in the lymphatic system

is the thoracic duct. It drains lymph fluid from the whole body below the diaphragm, the left side of the head, and the left side of the chest. The right lymphatic duct drains the rest of the body.

The largest organ in the immune system

is the spleen. As well as being a part of the immune system and a source of antibodies, the spleen breaks down and destroys old red blood cells as they pass through it.

The greatest source of lymph

is the liver. It produces nearly half of all the lymph in the body.

The widest part of the lymphatic system

is the cisterna chyli. Lymph from the legs and the digestive system drain into it.

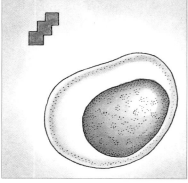

1 Lymphocyte recognizes enemy invader.

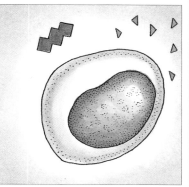

2 Lymphocyte makes antibodies against invader.

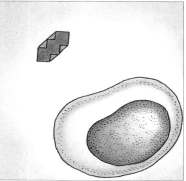

3 Antibodies attack invader and attach themselves to it.

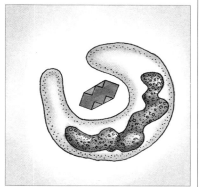

4 Other white cells arrive to clean up after the battle and to swallow up what's left of invader.

The only parts of the body without lymphatics

are the central nervous system, and the bones, cartilage and teeth.

Glands and Hormones

Many of the changes and activities in your body take place as a result of hormones travelling around in your bloodstream. Hormones are chemical messengers produced by your endocrine – or "ductless" – glands. These glands release their secretions directly into the bloodstream, unlike exocrine glands such as the salivary glands, which release saliva into the mouth down a duct.

There are two main types of hormone. One sort affects your day-to-day life and controls things such as the levels of water, sugar and salt in your body, or prepares the body for swift action in an emergency. The other sort has a more long-term effect and controls your growth and development over the years. The master gland controlling all this is the pituitary. Set deep in the brain, it not only produces its own hormones but it also regulates many of the other endocrine glands of the body.

EVOLUTION

The pineal gland has evolved from a primitive central eye. In some reptiles, the pineal actually reacts to light and can darken the skin when the creature is in bright light.

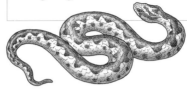

The most mysterious gland is the pineal. Lying deep in the brain and the shape of a pine cone, this part of the body seems to be a relic of what once was a third eye. It is still influenced by light and is most active during darkness. The hormone that it secretes may control types of behaviour that are associated with day and night – like when we feel hungry and when we want to sleep.

The smallest endocrine gland is the parathyroid. These four tiny pieces of tissue behind the thyroid gland play a major role in controlling the level of calcium in the body.

The gland that is biggest at birth (compared with the rest of the body) is the thymus. It produces hormones which are involved in the immune system that defends the body against attack by germs. The thymus seems to be able to train white blood cells to do this job. In babies and young children, the thymus is large, but by the time a person reaches old age, it will have shrunk away.

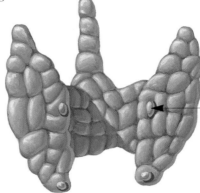

FLIGHT OR FIGHT

The hormone adrenalin causes the following things to happen to your body in response to danger – whether it's in the form of a hungry tiger or an important exam:
Your heart beats faster.
Your lungs take in more air.
Your liver releases extra glucose into the blood.
Blood is diverted from non-vital areas, such as your stomach, to your leg muscles.

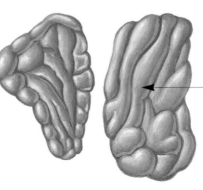

The glands that produce the most hormones are the two adrenals which sit on top of each kidney. They are really two glands in one. The outer part of the gland – the adrenal cortex – produces more than 24 steroid hormones. These help control body chemistry – salt and water control of the kidney is one example. The smaller centre of the gland – the adrenal medulla – produces hormones like adrenalin which automatically prepare the body for "flight or fight" in an emergency.

The most influential endocrine gland

is the pituitary. For its size – about the same as a pea – it is probably the most significant part of your brain. Because of the control it exerts over many of the other glands, it is often called "the conductor of the endocrine orchestra".

The largest pure endocrine gland

is the thyroid. Looking like a pinky-red butterfly, it sits across the windpipe and controls your metabolism – the activity level of your body. If your metabolism is working too fast, you become over-active; if it is too slow, you become sluggish.

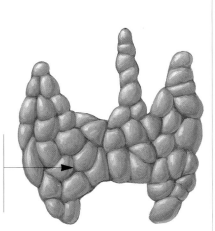

The longest endocrine gland

is the pancreas. Like the adrenals, it's really two glands in one. The hormone-producing, endrocrine part of its work is done by small areas of tissue called the Islets of Langerhans. These "islands" produce the hormones insulin and glucagon which control blood sugar levels.

The only veins with capillaries at either end

are those in the blood transport system that runs between the pituitary and the hypothalamus – the part of the brain which influences the pituitary.

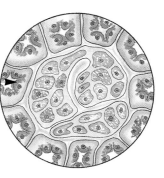

The glands with the most dramatic effect on teenagers

are the two ovaries in a girl, and the two testes in a boy. These begin to produce sex hormones in large quantities around puberty.

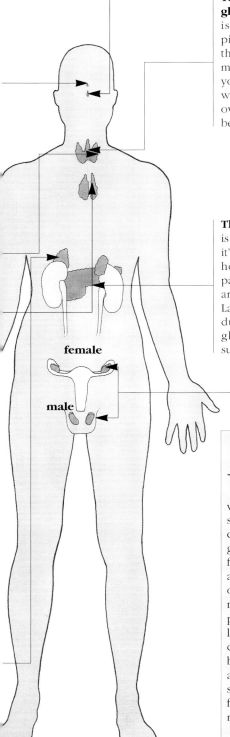

female

male

THE OVARIES AND TESTES

Until about the age of 11, the bodies of girls and boys are very similar in shape. Then, as sex hormones begin to be produced, their bodies change. In girls, the breasts get bigger, body fat increases around the thighs and hips, pubic hair grows, the ovaries begin to release eggs and menstruation starts. In boys, pubic and facial hair grows, the larynx enlarges so that the voice deepens, the shoulders become broader and the muscles larger, and the testes begin to produce sperm. At puberty, the male and female reproductive systems are ready to work fully.

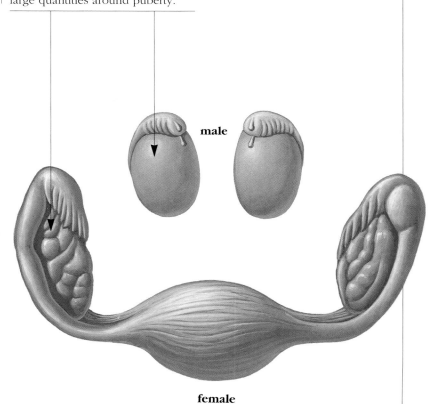

male

female

Bones, Joints and Ligaments

The bones of your skeleton are alive – not a bit like the white dusty objects dug up in graveyards. They contain a living collection of cells that grow, take in food, give out waste and need constant repair like any other parts of the body. They can be compared to a coral reef in the sea which has microscopic living creatures forming a huge underwater structure.

The outer layer of bone is hard and compact. This gives it strength. Inside this outer layer the bone is spongy and looks like a honeycomb. It's lighter than the outer bone but still very strong. The fact that much of the bone is not solid is important, as being light yet still strong is essential for ease of body movement. The centre of many bones contains a jelly-like material called marrow.

Although individual bones may appear hard and unyielding, together the 206 or so bones that make up a skeleton provide each of us with a flexible framework on which all the other organs of the body are supported. As well as a support, bones, helped by the muscles and tendons, provide the human body with a system of levers and pincers which enable our bodies to move at up to 35 kilometres per hour, and carry out a variety of tasks – some simple, such as picking up a pen, some more difficult, such as playing the piano. These are not the only functions of bones. For instance, small bones in the ear help you to hear by carrying sound vibrations to the brain. Other bones protect vital areas. Examples are the skull, protecting the brain, and the rib cage surrounding the heart and lungs.

The most rigid joints
are the "seams" between the flat bones that make up the skull. They do not move at all.

The largest tooth
is the first upper molar, which usually has three roots. Teeth are a specialised part of skin rather than bone even though they are so hard.

The longest tooth
is the upper canine.

Top three components of bone

1. 45% Minerals, like calcium phosphate. This material gives bone its hardness.

2. 30% Living tissue, such as blood vessels and bone cells.

3. 20% Water.

The largest sinus
within the skull is the maxillary sinus inside the cheekbone. Sinuses are useful because they lighten the weight of the skull and give resonance to the voice.

Joints and Ligaments

A place where bones meet is called a joint. Some joints can be moved by muscles and others are fixed. Joints that move are arranged to do so in different ways. Some work like hinges, and two examples are the knee and elbow. Others have developed like a ball and socket. Ball and socket joints give great all-round movement and good examples are the joints at the shoulder and hip. These enable your arms and legs to move freely in most directions. A universal joint, such as the wrist, is another way of providing a good range of movement. Within many of the mobile joints there is an "oiling" liquid called synovial fluid. This helps by lubricating the joint when it moves. A ligament is a strong, flexible non-elastic band which helps to hold two bones together at a joint.

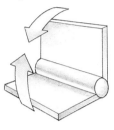

Hinge joint   Ball and socket joint   Universal joint

The shortest rib
is the first one. It is also the flattest and the most curvaceous of the twelve pairs of ribs. The second rib is more than twice its length.

The most fractured bone in the body
is the clavicle (collar bone). It is also the only "long" bone without a core of red marrow.

The most mobile joint
is your shoulder joint. The price for this great range of movement is that the shoulder is the joint in your body most likely to be "put out of joint" or dislocated by a violent fall.

31

Muscles and Tendons

Whether you are running, blinking or just standing still, you are using muscles. Some muscles – like the ones for running – are under your direct control. They are called voluntary muscles and you have about 650 of them, mostly attached to bones. Muscles tend to work in pairs. One muscle pulls a bone one way, then another pulls it back. Voluntary muscle is made up of bundles of fibres, each with a nerve ending embedded in it – it is along these nerves that your brain sends the orders to move. At the end of the muscle, the fibres join together in a tendon, the tough cord which anchors muscle to bone. Involuntary muscles work by themselves, outside your control. You can hear them working when your heart beats, or food gurgles on its way through your body.

The greatest combination of muscular movement and sensation anywhere in the body is found in the hand.

The most usual muscle movement of the wrist is the kind of action performed, for example, when knocking in a nail with a hammer. It's also performed when eating, drinking, washing, dressing, writing – and in just about every day-to-day task.

The overall champion for precise movement and sensation is the thumb. This is because it has a unique, saddle-shaped joint at its base, between the first metacarpal and the trapezium bone, which not only bends and straightens the thumb but also moves it across to touch the tips of the other fingers. Try five minutes of homework with your thumb taped to your first finger and you'll see how much humans rely on good muscle movement of the thumb.

The bone least likely to be broken is the scapula (shoulder blade). This is because it is very mobile and covered by strong muscles. The stability and great range of smooth movement of the bone depends on these muscles.

Your greatest source of body heat is in your muscles. Twelve people sitting and talking give off the same amount of heat as a one-bar electric fire! The brain uses this muscle heat to warm you up if you get cold by sending messages to your muscles to make them shiver and give off extra heat.

33

The Kidneys and Bladder

The two bean-shaped kidneys act as the washing machines for your blood. They filter waste and excess water out from the blood and form this into urine which drains out of your body from the bladder via the urethra. To find where your kidneys are, let your hands hang down your sides. The kidneys are in the middle of your back at the level of your elbows, where they are protected by your lower ribs and the surrounding padding of fat.

Over one litre of blood per minute flows down the renal arteries to the kidneys. This is a huge quantity of blood – about 20% of all that you have in your body. Once inside the kidney, each renal artery divides up into smaller and smaller branches. The blood that gushed into the kidneys now trickles much more slowly through these smaller vessels (capillaries). The purpose of this blood flow is to filter waste out of the blood. Each kidney has about one million filter units – or nephrons. Blood arrives at the tight knot of capillaries, called a glomerulus, within each nephron. It is surrounded by a cup-shaped structure called Bowman's capsule. The pressure of blood forces water, salts, urea and sugar from the blood through the membrane of this capsule and into a small tubule. In one day, about 165 litres of fluid from the blood passes through these membranes and into the tubules. It would be quite impractical to replace this amount by drinking if it were all passed out as urine. So the blood absorbs most of it back. The tubules are in close contact with the small capillaries and, as the fluid filtered out of the blood in the glomerulus passes down the tubules, 99% of it – substances useful to the body like water, sugar and salts – are taken back into the circulation. What remains in the tubules is a small amount of water and waste products such as urea. Rather like small rivers emptying into an estuary, the tubules all pour their urine into the renal pelvis. From here, the urine flows down the ureter into the bladder. Once the bladder starts to fill up, nerve sensors in the bladder wall detect that it's being stretched, and alert the brain by sending messages through the nervous system. This happens when about 300 millilitres of urine have collected.

EVOLUTION

Some desert animals, like the kangaroo rat of North America, can survive for many weeks without water. They have evolved to cope with their surroundings by cutting down on the amount of water lost from their bodies and making do with the water contained in food.

The most worm-like structure in your body
is the ureter. It moves like a worm as the muscles massage urine down into the bladder.

The largest reservoir of urine in the body
is the bladder. It's a collapsible muscular sac and can hold 1 litre of urine.

TOTAL DAILY OUTPUT OF WATER	
URINE	47%
SWEAT	31%
AIR BREATHED OUT	16%
FAECES	6%

The greatest percentage (90%) of kidney blood flow is to the cortex. All of the blood filter units (nephrons) are in this outer layer of the kidney.

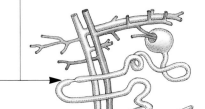

<table>
<tr><td></td></tr>
</table>

EXPERIMENT

The next time you have the chance to eat beetroot have a good helping and watch the urine you pass in the following hours. It's quite likely to be red because of the colouring of the beetroot. Your body gets rid of many other substances that you cannot see down this route.

The smallest groups of blood vessels in the kidney are the knots of capillaries in the glomerulus.

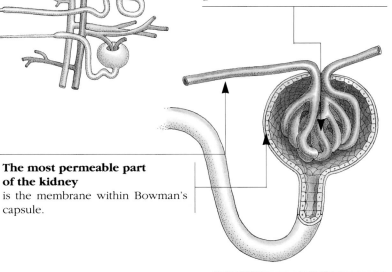

The "largest" ingredients of blood are the blood cells, protein molecules and platelets. Although tiny, they are still too big to pass through the membrane of Bowman's capsule. So they stay in the capillaries and do not enter the tubules.

The most permeable part of the kidney is the membrane within Bowman's capsule.

The highest of the two kidneys is on the left. The right kidney is lower because the liver pushes it down.

WATER CONTENT OF BODY ORGANS

GREY MATTER OF BRAIN	85%
BLOOD	80%
KIDNEY	80%
MUSCLE	75%
LIVER	70%
SKIN	70%
NERVOUS SYSTEM (WHITE MATTER)	70%
GRISTLE	60%
BONE	25–35%
FAT	20%

The greatest collection of tubules is within the inner region (medulla) of the kidney. It has been calculated that if you could lay all the tubules in the kidney end to end they would stretch for over 60 metres.

The greatest component of urine is water. It's about 95% water and 5% urea – a waste product made by the liver after protein in food has been digested. There are small amounts of other substances too. One of these, which comes from bile, gives urine its yellow colour.

Your body is 66% water. In fact you have enough water in your body to fill your Wellington boots four times (or an elephant's trunk once).

WATER CONTENT OF BODY FLUIDS

SWEAT	99%
SALIVA	97–99.5%
BILE	97%
URINE	95%
SEMEN	90%
BREAST MILK	88%

The longest urethra is found in the male. This tube that carries urine from the bladder to the outside world passes through the penis. In the male, the urethra is about 20 cm long and both urine and semen pass through it at different times. The female urethra is about 3–4 cm in length and carries only urine.

The Digestive System

The digestive system converts food into the energy and nutrients that fuel and build the cells of your body. When you think about food, or when you taste, smell, or chew it, this stimulates the six salivary glands to pour saliva into your mouth. When the food is swallowed, it passes down the oesophagus (gullet) and into the stomach. A flap called the epiglottis stops it going down the airway. The stomach churns up the food and adds its own digestive juices and hydrochloric acid. Then the food – which at this stage looks like a thick soup – is squirted on to the small intestine where yet more digestive juices are added to the mixture by the liver and pancreas. It is in the small intestine that most of the absorption of food into the bloodstream takes place. The remains of the food then pass into the large intestine, where much of the watery part of the "soup" is re-absorbed. If this part of the journey is speeded up for any reason, such as an infection, then there may not be time for this process to happen, and the waste is watery – what you know as diarrhoea. What's left of the food (faeces, which means "dregs" in Latin) arrives in the rectum about 24–36 hours after it has been eaten. From here, it passes to the outside world through the anus.

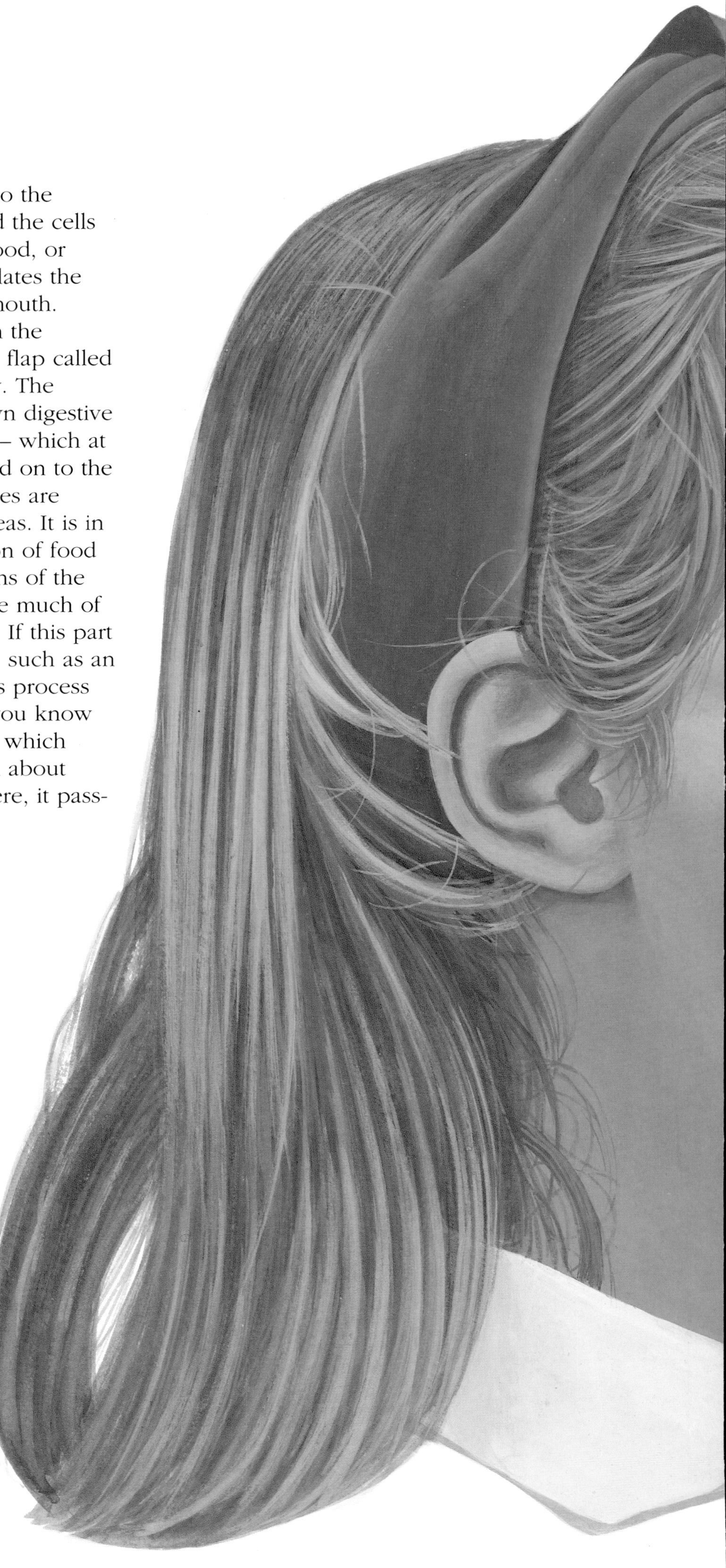

EXPERIMENT

Chew some cooked potato for a while and keep it in your mouth. Soon, the rather tasteless starch of the potato will begin to taste sweet. This is because a salivary enzyme called amylase has started to break the starch down into sugar ("amylum" is Latin for "starch"). This is the beginning of the whole digestive process.

The first stage in the process of digestion

takes place when your teeth chop the food into small pieces.

The thinnest parts of the lips

are the red parts where the colour of the blood is visible through the skin. The part of the body called the "lips" is actually much bigger than most people realize – they extend from the lowest part of the nose to the chin.

The Liver

A number of organs assist the main digestive system in the digestion of food. These are the teeth and tongue in the mouth, the salivary glands around the mouth, and the liver, gall bladder and pancreas in the abdomen. This varied collection of body parts contributes to the digestive process by chopping up food, adding saliva, bile and the chemicals – called enzymes – that help to break the food down so that it can be absorbed into the body. The liver is your largest internal organ, weighing around 1.5 kilos. The liver has a greater variety of jobs to do than any other organ of the body. Some experts credit it with over 500 functions. These fall into three main groups. It makes blood proteins. It breaks down foods into basic components, then either stores them or helps reassemble them into the body. It neutralises or destroys poisons like alcohol.

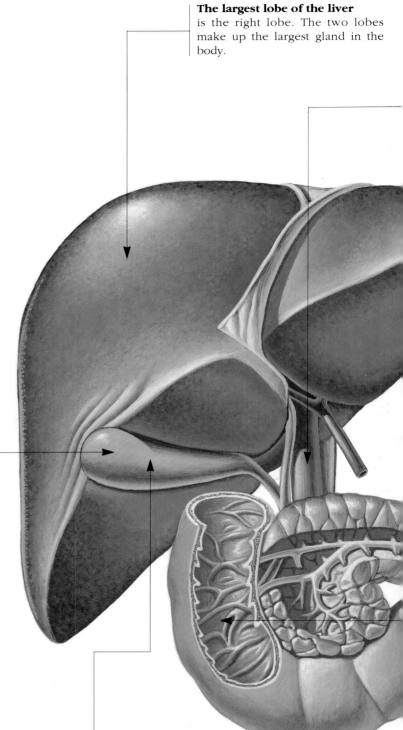

The largest lobe of the liver
is the right lobe. The two lobes make up the largest gland in the body.

The most digestive juices secreted in a day
come from the walls of the small intestine. In total, nearly 8 litres of such juices are made every day by your body.

The greenest substance in the body
is bile. In fact, it's a greeny-yellow liquid that looks like motor oil. The liver makes just under a litre a day. Bile acts like a detergent. It breaks up fats in food and is essential for the digestion of these fats into the body.

The largest collection of bile
is in the gall bladder, which has a 50 ml capacity. Bile is stored here until it is needed to work on fats in the intestine.

The greatest component of bile travelling down the bile duct
is water, which makes up 97%. The rest is 1% bile pigments (colouring), and 2% mineral salts and fatty acids.

EXPERIMENT

Volunteer for the washing-up next time there are greasy plates to clean. Washing-up liquid gets the fat off the plates and into the hot water in the same way that bile breaks down fat in food so that it can be absorbed into your body. This process is called emulsification, and you will see the small fat globules floating in the water as it happens.

The only vein in the body that has to do more than carry blood back to the heart

is the portal vein. It carries nutrients absorbed through the intestinal wall to the liver for processing.

The greatest food absorption in to your body

takes place across the walls of the jejunum. This 2.5 metre-long piece of small intestine joins the duodenum to the ileum. Because of all the food absorption taking place here the jejunum has a greater blood supply for its length than anywhere else in the intestines.

The largest and most complex transport system taking material to an organ

is found around the liver. Like other parts of the body, it has an artery to supply it with oxygenated blood, and a vein to take blood back to the heart. But it has a third source of blood, too – the portal vein that supplies it with venous (dark, deoxygenated) blood, and this gives it its unique dark red "liver" colour.

The most important gland for producing digestive enzymes

is the pancreas. Pinky-grey and shaped like a tadpole, it is 12–15 cm long. Through its system of ducts, it secretes digestive juices into the duodenum. These juices are alkaline, and help to neutralize the acid of the stomach. When they are first released by the pancreas, they are not active – rather like a grenade with the pin still in. The "pin" is only pulled out when the juices are safely in the duodenum with the food. This is a safety mechanism to prevent the pancreas digesting itself!

The widest opening in the wall of the duodenum

is where the bile duct and the pancreas release their digestive enzymes into it. It's often the only duct that does this, but some people also have a smaller extra duct carrying juices into the duodenum.

The gland which produces the widest variety of digestive enzymes

is the pancreas. It has at least one for every type of food – fat, protein and carbohydrate.

Digestive Juices Secreted Daily	
Small Intestine	2.5 litres
Stomach	2 litres
Pancreas	1.2 litres
Saliva	1 litre
Bile	0.7 litres

A New Life

A baby develops after a male sperm journeys to meet a female egg cell (ovum) and joins up with it. This union is called fertilization. It brings together the 23 chromosomes that the egg and the sperm each have to make one cell with 46 chromosomes – the number that all future body cells will have.

This cell implants itself into the lining of the womb of the mother and begins to grow into a new human being. From fertilization to birth will take about 280 days. At birth, the baby is perhaps the most amazing and complex creature ever to appear on Earth. Even death is not the end of this process, since our children and their genes – given to them by their mother and father – enable us to pass on our characteristics to future members of the human race.

The fastest human growth

is in the womb. From being a single cell to becoming a fully grown baby ready to be born, 50 cm long and weighing 3–4 kilos, takes only 40 weeks (9 months). If a baby continued to grow at this rate after birth, it would be around 2 km tall by its first birthday.

The only source of oxygen for a foetus floating in fluid inside the womb

is down the umbilical cord. The cord is made up of two arteries and one vein. Unlike anywhere else in the body except in the lungs, these arteries carry deoxygenated blood, and the veins oxygen-rich blood – which shows how the lungs and placenta do very similar jobs.

The organ that exists only in pregnancy

is the placenta. It develops on the inside wall of the uterus. Food and oxygen from the mother are passed from the placenta to the baby in the blood supply along the umbilical cord.

The muscle that can change the most (in the female body)

is the uterus. Usually, this hollow organ is only about the size of a duck's egg and weighs about 30 g. However, when a woman becomes pregnant and a baby begins to grow inside the uterus, it increases in size to weigh over 1 kilo.

The widest part of the foetus

is the head. This is the part that usually comes out of the mother's body first. The female pelvis is wider than the male's to allow the the baby's head to pass through.

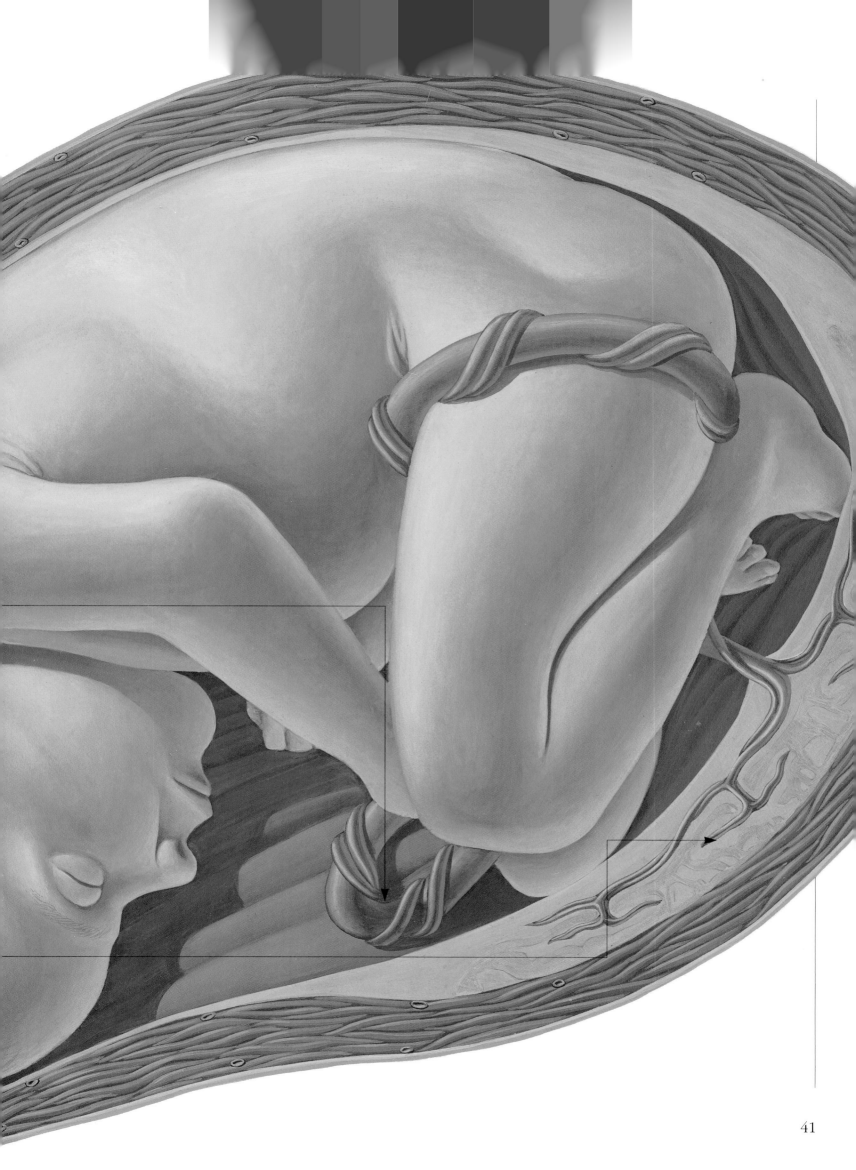

41

Last Records

BOWEL GASES	TOP THREE
1 CARBON DIOXIDE	
2 HYDROGEN	
3 METHANE	

SPEED OF ACTIONS	
NERVE MESSAGES	360 KPH
RUNNING (MALE SPRINTER)	43.37 KPH
RUNNING (FEMALE SPRINTER)	39.56 KPH
MARCHING	5.7 KPH
BLOOD LEAVING THE HEART	3.6 KPH
FLUID MOUTH TO STOMACH	0.72 KPH
BANANA SLUG (FASTEST MOLLUSC)	0.02642 KPH
SPERM	0.00021 KPH

The commonest sound made by the human voice
is "a" – like the "a" in "father". No language is without this sound.

The coolest parts of your body
are the fingers and feet. Blood reaching your toes as you read this is probably around room temperature.

The hottest part of your body
is in the centre of the brain. This is because the brain receives a large percentage (16%) of the blood leaving the heart and this blood is hot. The chest, where this blood comes from, is not as warm as you might expect because of the cooler blood returning to it from the outer-most parts of the body.

LIFESPAN OF BODY CELLS	
LINING DUODENUM	3–4 DAYS
SKIN CELLS	7 DAYS
WHITE BLOOD CELLS	14 DAYS
SMELL NEURONES	60 DAYS
RED BLOOD CELLS	120 DAYS
BONE CELLS	10–30 YEARS
NERVE CELLS	A LIFETIME

LOUDEST BODY NOISES	
JET TAKING OFF	130 DECIBELS
SCREAM	128 DECIBELS
WHISTLE	122.5 DECIBELS
SHOUT	119 DECIBELS
SNORE	90 DECIBELS
NORMAL SPEECH	60 DECIBELS
WHISPER	20 DECIBELS
SOFTEST NOISE	10 DECIBELS

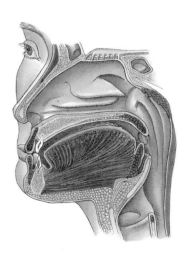

SPEEDS OF AIR MOVEMENT	
FASTEST SNEEZE	167 KPH
HURRICANE	117.5 KPH
COUGH	100 KPH
HICCUP	80 KPH
PANTING	35 KPH
LAUGH	25 KPH
SPEECH	18 KPH
YAWN	15 KPH
SNORING	10-12 KPH
BREATHING WHEN ASLEEP	8 KPH

The greatest range of hearing belongs to babies. Sound comes in waves that are measured in hertz (Hz) – the faster the waves, the greater the number of hertz – and the higher the sound. Babies can hear sounds in the range of 20,000 Hz. As we get older, we lose the ability to hear at these higher ranges. Most normal speech is in the 250–4,000 Hz range (bats, whom we cannot hear, emit sounds in the 90,000 range). In an opera by the composer Mozart, the singer is required to sing a low D (73.4 Hz). This is the lowest note in classical music.

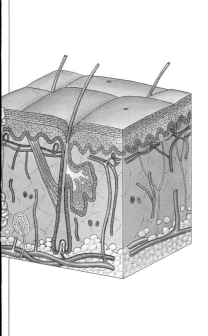

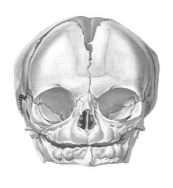

END-TO-END LENGTHS	
BLOOD VESSELS	96,000 KILOMETRES
NERVES	75 KILOMETRES
KIDNEY TUBULES	64 KILOMETRES
SWEAT GLANDS	48 KILOMETRES
TESTES TUBULES	0.8 KILOMETRES

WEIGHTS OF ORGANS	TOP TEN
SKIN	4000 G
LIVER	1600 G
BRAIN	1400 G
RIGHT LUNG	625 G
LEFT LUNG	570 G
PLACENTA	500 G
HEART	280 G
SPLEEN	200 G
KIDNEY	150 G
PANCREAS	85 G

SURFACE AREAS OF PARTS OF BODY	
SMALL BOWEL	OVER 200 SQ METRES
LUNGS	143 SQ METRES
SKIN	1.8 SQ METRES
CEREBRAL CORTEX	0.22 SQ METRES
SMELLING SURFACE	0.025 SQ METRES

Index

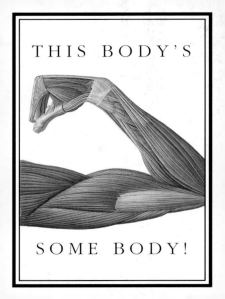